Fuerteventura Tourism
Touristic Information

Author
John Knight

Copyright Notice

Copyright © 2017 Global Print Digital
All Rights Reserved

Digital Management Copyright Notice. This Title is not in public domain, it is copyrighted to the original author, and being published by **Global Print Digital**. No other means of reproducing this title is accepted, and none of its content is editable, neither right to commercialize it is accepted, except with the consent of the author or authorized distributor. You must purchase this Title from a vendor who's right is given to sell it, other sources of purchase are not accepted, and accountable for an action against. We are happy that you understood, and being guided by these terms as you proceed. Thank you

First Printing: 2017.

ISBN: 978-1-912483-43-3

Publisher: Global Print Digital.
Arlington Row, Bibury, Cirencester GL7 5ND
Gloucester
United Kingdom.
Website: www.homeworkoffer.com
.

Table of Content

About Fuerteventura 1
History 3
   Fuerteventura History & Geography 3
Fuerteventura Culture 11
Tourism 21
   Things to See and Do in Fuerteventura 21
   Activities in Fuerteventura 24
   Nature & Wildlife in Fuerteventura 30
   Nightlife 33
   Things to Do: Activities and Attractions 36
      The American Star has now sunk into history 36
      Beaches 37
      Fuerteventura Fishing 42
      Home Making on Sunny Fuerteventura. 45
      Shopping on Fuerteventura 47
      Touring on Fuerteventura. 50
      Walking on Fuerteventura 51
      Fuerteventura sailing 53
      Scuba Diving, Fuerteventura 55
      Snorkelling in Fuerteventura 56
      Fuerteventura surfing 57
      Windsurfing on Fuerteventura 59
      Fuerteventura Kiteboarding 61
      Golf on Fuerteventura 64
      Running in Fuerteventura 66
      Walking on Fuerteventura 68
      Watersports on Fuerteventura 70
      Cycling and mountain biking on Fuerteventura 71
      Achipencos, Fuerteventura 73
      Fuerteventura Feaga. 74
      Events and fiestas on Fuerteventura 75
         Battle of Tamasite 79
         XiX International Kite Festival, Festival International de Cometas , Playa del Burro 81

    A Fuerteventura Wedding, one couples Experience 82
    Christmas in Fuerteventura, a guide to the festive season 85
    Canarian Wrestling, Lucha Canaria on Fuerteventura..................... 88
Visit a lava cave 89
Restaurants in Fuerteventura... 97
Cruising around the Canaries 99
Fuerteventura, Wildlife and Nature 101
Lanzarote 103

Tour *104*
2-Day Scuba Course with Open-Water Dive................................. 105
Beginner Scuba Diving Lesson in Caleta de Fuste....................... 106
Catamaran Cruise to Playa de Papagayo 107
Fuerteventura Oasis Park 107
Freebird Catamaran Tour to Isla de Lobos 108
Full-Day Trip to Fuerteventura 109
Full-Day Trip to Fuerteventura's Sand Dunes............................... 110
Glass-Bottom Boat Cruise to 3 Islands 111
Glass-bottomed Sailing Adventure 113
Go-Kart Experience at Gran Karting Club 113
Grand Tour of Lanzarote 114
Lobos Island Full-Day Tour with Lunch 116
Off-Road Safari along Fuerteventura's Northern Coast 116
Off-Road Safari along Fuerteventura's Southern Coast 118
Offshore Kayak & Snorkeling Adventure...................................... 119
Rancho Texas Lanzarote Park Admission 120
Scuba Diving Introduction off the Lanzarote Coast..................... 120
Small-Group Cruise Aboard a Traditional Turkish Gulet 121
Ultimate Dune Buggy Adventure.. 122
Submarine Tour 124
Small-Group Fuerteventura Sightseeing Tour 125

Other Information *126*
Twinkle Trust Animal Aid.. 126
Health Matters on Fuerteventura 129
Fuerteventura Transport 133
Emergencies 137
Holidays for those with mobility and other disabilities in Fuerteventura..139

Touring on Fuerteventura. 140
Long Term Accommodation Fuerteventura 142
Travel Information... 145
Events in Fuerteventura 148

About Fuerteventura

Fuerteventura, the sunny Grand Canary Island, is a unique and vibrant island renowned for its reputation as a fabulous sun holiday destination. The island boasts an unforgettable coastline, volcanic semi-desert terrain and picturesque white-washed villages. Visitors to Fuerteventura will enjoy not only the Spanish and traditional flair of the capital Puerto del Rosario but the laid back lifestyle and myriad of markets, local museums, all within the setting of breathtaking natural beauty (over 300 days of sun a year, archipelago islands, ocean, mountain ranges, and white sandy beaches).

In both Fuerteventura's urban and rural areas you will countless reminders of the island's rich history such as historic churches, windmills, museums, and anscestral homes. You will also find no shortage of water sports and outdoor activities. Expect world-class kite and windsurfing, scuba diving, swimming, mountain biking, hiking and of course sunbathing.

Fuerteventura is undeniably an island that balances tourism with its local lifestyle and traditions and few islands can boast the stunning beaches and scenery, cultural museums, fantastic local eateries and enough festivals to fill up an entire calendar year as can Fuerteventura. In short, Fuerteventura is an exciting location for all visitors.

History
Fuerteventura History & Geography

The least developed of the Canaries, Fuerteventura has largely escaped the indiscriminate coastal development of the other islands of the archipelago. With year round sunshine and an average temperature of 20 degrees centigrade its equable dry climate and endless beaches make it the perfect destination for holidays of all kinds, from sheltered safe beaches ideal for families with small children, to wide open bays with some of the best surfing waves in the Canaries.

Rainfall is rare, for with no high mountains, the moisture laden north easterly trade wind pass unimpeded over the island. Its dry interior, a striking landscape of ancient volcanoes, dry steppe and rolling sandy hills lined with stone terraces has small picturesque villages and some of the oldest churches of the entire archipelago. The locals are used to a relaxed slow pace of life, and are friendly to visitors in a genuine unspoiled sort of way

Where?

This is the second largest island of the Canaries, located at latitude 28° 27' N, longitude: 13° 51' W and measuring 110 km (75 miles) from north to south and 20 km (15 miles) at its widest point.

With a surface area of 1600 sq km (620 sq miles) Fuerteventura has a resident population of only 100,000. Most people live and work in the two tourist centres of Morro Jable and Corralejo, and in the administrative capital of Puerto Rosario in the centre of the eastern coast. The southern end of the island is separated from the north by a long strip of high sand dunes - the beaches here on the eastern side are amongst the best in the entire Atlantic. Here a 3 kilometre (1.8 mile) long tidal lagoon and the strong northerly trade winds make perfect conditions for wind and kite surfing - the world Championships are held at Playa Sotavento every year. The main southern resort of Morro Jable is popular with German tourists and is fronted by a long promenade lined with hotels, a cycle and running path and a newly created marine wetland area which backs the 3 kilometre long beach of white sand.

At the northern end of the island Corralejo, once a tiny fishing village, is now a sprawling tourist town with a large range of hotels and apartment blocks. Just outside the town are spectacular dunes of sand so fine it flows like water between your toes. A protected natural park, the sheltered and endless beaches here slope gently into the sea, and are a perfect place for family and small children.

Just off Corralejo lies the small uninhabited island of Isla de los Lobos named after the seals which once bred on its sandy beaches.

Now a protected natural area it offers glimpses of the volcanic history of this ancient island, with a rugged interior of black lava eroded into fantastic shapes by millions of years of wind and sand erosion.

Tiny and tough flowering plants endemic to the island bring unexpected colour to the landscape, and sea water lagoons and wetlands are thronged with visiting birds migrating to Europe and back from Africa every year. The waters around the Isla de Lobos are part of the nature reserve, and offer wonderful snorkelling and diving locations.

The western coast of Fuerteventura is a wild unspoiled land of high cliffs, and deserted beaches pounded by huge waves which roll unimpeded from the distant shores of America some 4000 km (2,400 m) to the west. At Cofete, the 5 km beach is one of the stars of the newly created Biosphere Reserve, its virgin cliffs of volcanic rock some of the highest on the island. Walking here, it is possible to get glimpses of the days when the islands were undiscovered, inhabited only by the Majoreros, the original indigenous people of the island, thought to have come to Fuerteventura from the African mainland in the first two millennia BC.

Who?

The first inhabitants of the island were known as the Majoreros - named after the original kingdom of Maxorata, at the northern end of the island. Thought to have been of Berber origin, early accounts by the first Spanish explorers describe them as a warlike fierce people.

Historians think that there were about 1000 Majoreros in total when the island was first settled by Europeans in the early 15th century, descendants of slaves brought from Mauretania in the first two millennia BC to harvest lichens much prized in the making of dyes. Today the only trace of the original Majoreros are more than 250 foot shaped carvings known as podomorphs, on the summit of the ancient volcano of Tindaya.

The first Spanish Conquistador to discover and occupy the island was the Norman Jean de Béthencourt in 1405, who quickly subdued and enslaved the indigenous Majoreros. He established the first settlement at Betancuria, in a hidden valley protected from pirate attack close the west coast, with an abundant water supply.

Over the following three hundred years the island was slowly settled throughout by peasant farmers who worked the arid lands using donkeys and camels. Fuerteventura became known as the granary of the Canary islands, with wheat and corn grown on the fertile plains and on the rolling hills lined with painstakingly constructed stone terraces.

By the 18th century the island was ruled by the Coroneles - literally the colonels - local militia leaders appointed by Spain who ruled the island virtually as their private fiefdom. Their headquarters - a large imposing fortified manor house surrounded by outhouses is known as La Casa de los Coroneles and this building still stands to this day in the inland village of La Oliva.

In the early 19th century the Coroneles finally ceded their powers to the Spanish state and in 1912, along with the other islands of the archipelago Fuerteventura was run by its Cabildo - a semi autonomous council - from the administrative capital in Puerto Rosario. Life on the island was never easy, and during periods of protracted drought islanders would emigrate to the other islands or further afield to South America, Cuba and the Peninsula - as islanders call Spain.

Today, practically no farming takes place on the island and the land lies fallow, although some small scale farms use both traditional and modern irrigation methods to produce the richly flavoured tomatoes and small potatoes which are a speciality of the Canary Islands.

The island's population mirrors its prosperity - with 11,000 registered in the census of 1900 growing to a peak of 129,000 in 2006. As a major holiday destination, with 1.4 million visitors registered in 2006, most islanders work in the tourist sector but unemployment is rising as the global recession impacts the Spanish economy. However many islanders think that the slow down in the world economy may have a long term benefit for the island, as many new planned developments which would have had a severe impact on the fragile ecology of the coast have been abandoned. Today the Patronato - the governing council of the island - is committed to sustainable tourism, and is taking measures to ensure that the island avoids the pitfalls of mass tourism experienced by other islands of the archipelago.

The recent award of Biosphere Reserve status for the entire island by UNESCO is a further accolade for Fuerteventura - and recognises the unique marine, coastal and terrestrial attributes of the island. There are plans now to make the entire western coast a National Park and so ensure that this extraordinarily beautiful and unique area remains in its virgin state for generations to come

What?

Fuerteventura is the oldest of the Canary islands, first created between 30 and 70 million years ago when huge volcanic eruptions spewed lava through a hot spot between the tectonic plates of South America and Africa. The island of lofty volcanoes stood alone in the Atlantic for millions of years until more eruptions created the remaining islands of the archipelago. The last active volcano fell silent 4 million years ago on Fuerteventura and the high mountains have long eroded away, the ancient volcanic plugs and craters still standing as jagged hills of black rock amongst wide sweeping landscapes of dry steppe.

The highest point at Mt Jandia is barely 800 metres (2,600 feet) above sea level and so the moisture-laden north easterly trades pass unimpeded, creating an arid climate with rain falling rarely each year. But the dry semi-desert landscape has its own rugged beauty, with tiny villages and hamlets of small flat roofed houses scattered across the plains of the interior.

On the eastern coast between the larger tourist towns, small fishing villages still retain their original character, with boats drawn up on beaches of both white and black lava sand. To the west the wild coast is more than 100 kilometres (60 miles) long and is virtually uninhabited, the rugged high cliffs streaked with ancient strata and folds of rock. The island is a geologists paradise, for practically every volcanic rock formation known to man can be seen, with some of the oldest rock on earth clearly visible in the chaotic jumble of folded strata and ancient uplifted sea shores. More than 50 sites of paleontological interest have been mapped on the island - giving scientists the chance to study and understand the complex climatic changes which have taken place over millions of years.

Fuerteventura Culture

Fuerteventura is closely bound up with the sea. Its first inhabitants were thought to have been slaves brought to the island from Mauretania in the first two millennia BC to harvest lichens used to make dyes. Their descendants lived more or less undisturbed until pirates and explorers from the European mainland first landed here in the 12th and 13th centuries. Finally claimed for Spain by Jean de Béthencourt in 1405 the island then became an important staging post for ships on the voyage to the New World. In the following centuries waves of both immigration and emigration brought in many cultural influences, and today the island has its own distinctive identity; the Majoreros, as islanders still call themselves, are proud of their long tradition of being a resolute, independent and capable people.

Fuerteventurans still refer to themselves as majoreros, a term that already introduces you to a little of the island's history and culture, as it comes from the Guache people who originally inhabited the

Canaries. But there's a lot more to learn about this volcanic land and its majoreros. There's no better place to discover Fuerteventura's story than in its oldest towns, and particularly in Betancuria. Named after its founder Jean de Béthencourt, who conquered the island in 1405, Betancuria is the island's most historic village, evident in its old-fashioned streets lined by squat, whitewashed homes. It is here that you can also dig deeper into the island's past by visiting the Museum of Archeology and Ethnography.

Other time-weathered towns of note include Pájara with is 17th-century church look closely at its unique façade, which is said to have Aztec influences (not surprising given the islands' Latin American ties). You'll also want to pay a visit to the central village of Antigua, home to an old mill next to which sits the Museo de Queso, or the Cheese Museum, a great way to learn more about the island's gastronomy.

Speaking of cheese, Fuerteventura is known throughout Spain for its majojero cheese. This thick, creamy delicacy is made from goats' milk a logical ingredient given the region's tradition of goat farming. While in these parts, you'll also want to try other Canarian specialties, including crowd favorite papas arrugadas, the wrinkly potatoes that typically come served with a side of both red and green mojo (punchy sauces that can make just about anything taste like heaven). And given that these islands are surrounded by nothing but sea, you'd be wise to bring an appetite for local seafood, ranging from the white fish vieja to the shellfish snail relatives called lapas.

If you're seeking a more up-close-and-personal encounter with Fuerteventuran culture, though, your best bet is to visit the island during its biggest religious pilgrimage, called La Romería de La Peña. This is when, every September, people from all around the island (and even beyond) make their way to the inland town of Vega de Río Palmas, where they pay tribute to the Virgin of the Peña. It's a very religious gathering but also an event in which other cultural traditions are celebrated as well.

Food and drink on Fuerteventura
Our products are all locally grown and are fresh and healthy - our fish and meat could not be more so..."

Locally grown vegetables are rich in flavour and the goats' milk and meat are renowned for their flavour and quality. The waters around the island teem with fish, and the rocky coast provides many kinds of shellfish. The cuisine of the island is simple - but the ingredients are of the best quality - producing a winning combination.

Some dishes to try:

Goat in all forms - from rich stews to tender grilled kid chops - try the gofio escaldado - stock thickened with toasted corn flour and kid meat.

Gofio - this speciality of the island is made from toasted corn and wheat flour. In the past when bread was a luxury eaten only at special occasions gofio would have been a staple for every meal. Mixed with milk it was served at breakfast ; blended with fish or meat stock and vegetables it would have provided the base for the main meal of the day, before being served again with milk for supper. Today it is used to thicken and flavour soups, stocks and stews. Try the Escaldon de Gofio de caldo de pescado - a rich fish stew made with gofio and vegetables.

Papas arrugadas - Most dishes are accompanied by these tiny delicious potatoes cooked in very salty water and then baked for a few minutes and eaten whole in their wrinkled skins.

Mojos - sauces made from olive oil, vinegar, herbs, and a selection of spices are served with every meal. The red mojo is made using peppers and can be very spicy for everyone has their own recipe. Green mojo is based on parsley or coriander and is mostly eaten with fish dishes.

Fish of all kind are on the menu - but try the Vieja - a parrot fish which is common around the islands. The cheapest fish on the menu, it has one of the best flavours and a firm white flesh.

Sea bass and bream too are often on the menu - with tuna and some times swordfish depending on availability. But you can always be assured that the fish will be fresh - for the sea is never far away here.

The variety of seafood is extraordinary, from prawns to massive mussels, crabs, and lobster. The paella of Fuerteventura with fresh natural ingredients is of excellent quality and is always reasonably priced.

The goats cheese of Fuerteventura (Queso Majorero) is sought after in the Canaries and the Spanish mainland. The goat milk from which the Queso Majorero is made is renowned for its high fat content and thick creamy texture. The cheese is often served sprinkled with olive oil, or with gofio - the toasted corn flour contrasting smoothly with the crisp taste of the cheese. Natural sea salt, produced in the traditional way in salt pans along the eastern coast at Las Salinas is often mixed into the cheese in the production process - giving it a distinctive flavour.

Many small restaurants in the country areas are family run and pride themselves on the simple excellence of their cuisine. When on the coast have the ultimate Fuerteventura experience of lunch in a cofradia - the fishermen's cooperative where the catch is landed and auctioned each day.

Here the fish will have been landed hours before, and prices are very reasonable. Where better to sit in the shade with a cold beer or chilled glass of white wine overlooking the port as boats return from fishing.

Restaurant list

- Gran Tarajal Cofradia, Recinto Portuario de Gran Tarajal, Tarajal (Tel: 928162074)
- El Horno restaurant, Carretera general 91, Villaverde (Tel: 928 868671)
- Café Marcos Gastronomy bar, Carratera General, Villaverde (Tel: 0928868285)
- El Verrol Cafeteria, c.León Castillo, Puerto del Rosario (Tel: 928 530 345)
- La Flor de Antgua Restaurant, c. Obispo 43, Antigua (Tel: 928878168)
- El Chinchorro Bar, Plaza Cirilo López 5, Morro Jable

Fuerteventura Museum Trail
There are excellent museums and interpretation centres throughout Fuerteventura which cover all aspects of life in the island.

At the Alcogida Eco-Museum a typical country hamlet has been restored to its hey day in the early part of this century. Weavers, a stone mason, a tinsmith and a potter are working on site in the collection of houses which give an insight into the simple living conditions of only two generations ago. Villagers then relied on their own skills to provide most of their needs. The houses of stone and thatch are surrounded by stone walled corrals complete with donkeys and camels which were used to pull ploughs and transport produce until only 50 years ago.

At the Cueva del Llano Centro de Interpretacion, an extraordinary tunnel made by rapid flowing lava stretches far underground - the vivid remnant of an eruption which took place many millions before One of the largest lava tubes in the northern hemisphere, you can walk for nearly a kilometre through the still darkness, the arching walls still bearing the marks of the rapid flow of molten rock. There is also a permanent resident to the tube, a tiny blind spider which is endemic to the cave.

The Museo de la Sal at Las Salinas - complete with the skeleton of a sperm whale - is set above salt pans close to the sea which are lined with blinding white piles of salt crystals in the strong sun.

Inside a display tells of the importance of salt to Fuerteventura when it was the sole means of preserving food and was used as a currency to barter for goods.

At the Molinos de Antigua another restored windmill stands in a visitors centre.

Here permanent and touring exhibitions are popular with islanders - and include displays of artefacts and bones of the earliest Majoreros on the island dating back more than a thousand years. There is also a craftwork shop with locally made items- from distinctive pottery of red clay mixed with volcanic soil to woven baskets and panama hats. Proceeds go directly to the artisans who made the articles on display.

At Los Molinos in the pretty village of Tefia a working windmill - one of the few survivors of the hundreds which once dotted the landscape here - grinds gofio, the toasted meal of corn and wheat

At the top of the tower, miller Jorge Rodriguez will explain the process of toasting and then grinding the corn as the huge sails outside spin slowly in the strong trade wind. You can taste the freshly ground gofio - the fine flour that pours out from the wooden chute beneath the grind stones

At the Museo de Pesca Tradicional on the lovely windswept point of Punta Tostón near the fishing village of Cotillo the fishing museum has a vivid display of video, photographs, and recordings set in the lighthouse keeper's restored home. You can listen to the wife of a fisherman describing life on the coast two generations ago at a time when money was scarce and when fish was used to barter. Above the museum stand two light houses, the oldest built in 1897. From the tower there are wonderful views across the reefs to the high breaking rollers of the Atlantic.

Folklore Music

The traditional folk music of the Canary Islands, Folklore, can be heard at the major festivals and at other special events. At the big Fiestas there are often groups representing their respective Islands - each of which have their own traditional costumes.

A less formal type of Folklore music can heard at several bars and bodegas (usually away from the main resorts) where Locals get together for impromptu "sessions"

Lucha Canaria

Lucha Canaria is a type of wrestling - somewhat reminiscent of Sumo - that is popular in the Islands. It is a team sport with individuals taking turns in individual bouts. The Bouts starts with the participants gripping each other's shorts, the object of the game being to push your opponent onto the ground.

Eating and Drinking habits

As in southern Spain, there is a Siesta between One and Four in the afternoon when locals will take their main meal of the day. Spanish people then eat a smaller meal in the late evening - often after Nine o'Clock at night

Spanish people like to go out late and a typical Saturday night out might not kick off until about Midnight. Northern Europeans are often the only ones only people in Discos or Disco Bars before 1AM.

Dress

The Spanish like to dress well and although the Locals of Fuerteventura are a little more relaxed than their cousins from the Peninsula (Mainland Spain), they are still better turned out better than most tourists. Groups of Spanish Tourists can easily be spotted as they take their evening stroll due to their immaculate dress.

Religion

Spain is an overwhelmingly Catholic country, although your average Spaniard probably follows a liberal interpretation of the religion and Mass attendances are continually declining.

That said, all of the major Catholic calendar events are observed, Christmas is of special importance with the 6th of January being the most important day (rather than the 25th).

Tourism

Actually Fuerteventura has turned in one of the most popular destinations in Spain and also in Europe according with the online travel and tourism statistics. Some of the arguments for get that are the magnificent and impressive beaches, exquisite gastronomy, people hospitality, the unique and exceptional climate and a lenght etcetera.

Things to See and Do in Fuerteventura

3.5 kilometres off the Corralejo, the island is a Protected Natural Area, and has excellent beaches, walking and cycling paths, plus good snorkelling in rocky hidden coves. There are regular boat trips to the island from Corralejo, and a small restaurant can supply lunches and cold drinks. There are many interesting birds and plants here, some endemic to the island, and on the northern side a large wetland is used by waders and ducks on the annual migration route between

Europe and Africa. The island also has good surf - with one of the longest rides on the entire island of Fuerteventura.

Dolphins, pilot whales and hammerhead sharks are regular visitors to the waters close to the island.

Dunes of Corralejo

These extraordinary dunes of white fine sand extend to the south of the town of Corralejo and are a protected nature park. Beaches here are so long that they are never crowded, and the shallow shelving water is ideal for young children. There is easy access from the road which runs about 500 metres behind the beach.

The ancient volcano of Tindaya

Permission has to be obtained to climb this ancient volcanic core close to La Oliva. At the summit strange foot shaped incisions are carved into the rock -created by the original Majoreros who lived on the island a thousand years before European discovery. On clear days the snow covered peak of Tenerife more than 100 miles to the west can be seen from here with views of Gran Canaria and Lanzarote - the nearest island for the archipelago. Walkers must obtain a permission from the Environmental Agency in Puerto Rosario and be accompanied by an natural park guard.

Punta de Jandia and Cofete

The extraordinary wild beach of Cofete in the Jandia Natural Park on the west coast can be reached only by a rough unsurfaced road which leads out from the port of Morro Jable and climbs over the central rocky spine of the island. Park rules state that drivers must stay on the marked track which has some of the best views on the island as it corkscrews down over the mountains to the sea. The beach is more than 5 kilometres long beneath high black cliffs, so there will always be space for those prepared to walk away from the parking area.

The loggerhead turtle hatchery is located here, and it is hoped that within ten years female turtles will once again return to the beach to lay their eggs for the first time in nearly a century. Continue west on the track to Punta de Jandia and the lighthouse which stands at the westernmost tip of the island. At Puerto de la Cruz - a small fishing village and fishing port on the leeward side of the peninsula two small restaurants have excellent menus of seafood and fish. Try the delicious escaldon de gofio de caldo de pescado - a rich stew of fish in a stock thickened with gofio - the distinctive toasted corn flour of the island.

Cotillo

This pretty fishing village on the north coast has lovely surfing beaches below high cliffs - swimmers have to be careful here for there are many currents on this western coast. In the tiny fishing port below the village fishermen regularly land their catches of tuna and sardines. Just beyond the village at the Punta de Tostón rocky sun warmed pools make for good snorkelling or swimming.

Casa de los Coroneles

In the inland village of La Oliva stands the much restored Casa de los Coroneles, a very distinctive fortified manor house of the mid 17th century, built by the militia leaders who virtually ran the island as their own private fiefdom for nearly two centuries.

The interior courtyard with a high broad balcony made of canary pine is a cool retreat in the heat of the day. The ground floor of the house is now used for exhibitions of paintings and photographs by artists from the island:

Activities in Fuerteventura

Surrounded by sea, with more than 150 excellent beaches - some of which are the longest in the Atlantic - and with an interior of rolling plains and hills Fuerteventura offers a wide range of activity-based holidays for both individuals and families.

Diving

The volcanic mass of Fuerteventura rises sheer from the sea bottom which in places is more than 1 kilometre (3,300 feet) deep. With a water temperature ranging from 16 to 25 degrees centigrade and visibility up to 50 metres (150 feet) the island has some of the best diving conditions in the archipelago and there are many dive spots suitable for both beginners and advanced divers. Well equipped dive centres and schools in the main centres of Corralejo, Caleta de Fuste and Jandia offer PADI training courses in a variety of languages including Japanese.

The underwater landscapes of lava sculpted into fantastic shapes, with caves, grottoes and sandy stretches teem with fish. Barracuda, Parrot fish, squid and octopus are amongst the many species that can be seen in the clear waters and on drift dives the lava walls encrusted with corals and anemones are a perfect habitat for large moray eels and groupers. The Isla de los Lobos, a protected natural area surrounded by shallow clear water is a popular diving area just off the town of Corralejo. Spotted rays, dolphins, pilot whales and hammerhead sharks are often sighted here. On the rugged west coast large underwater caves and overhangs in the volcanic rock provide some of the best diving on the island, but this area, with strong currents and high seas, is for the experienced diver only.

Snorkelling

The many beaches on the east coast and some of the sheltered rocky coves of the north coast are ideal for snorkelling. In the rocky pools and lagoons water temperatures can rise to 25 degrees, and with the clear visibility, bright colours and many fish species divers compare snorkelling Fuerteventura favourably with the Caribbean. Islanders often carry fins and a mask in their cars as a matter of course, sometimes catching octopus and squid (only on Saturdays and Sundays in controlled areas) for the weekend paella. Moray eels, grouper, squid, octopus, brightly coloured star fish, and the ubiquitous parrot fish are a common sight for snorkelers around the island.

Surfing

The northern coast of the island close to Corralejo and the pretty village of Cotillo has some of the best and crispest waves of the Atlantic. The warm waters mean that lightweight wetsuits are sufficientalthough some hardier souls surf in Bermuda shorts. Surf schools offer courses for beginners in the safe waters off the shallow shelving beaches where beginners can hone their skills before venturing out to take on the bigger rollers. A good wave is more or less guaranteed year round although the best and biggest are in autumn and winter. There are some long rides available one of the favourites being to catch a wave of the northern side of the Isla de los

Lobos and to ride it for the entire length of the island. It does entail though a long walk or paddle back up the coast!

Wind and kite surfing

The eastern coast of the island, with strong north easterly trade winds has the perfect combination for kite and wind surfing, for both expert and beginner. The Playa Sotavento at Costa Calma on the southern end of the island is world renowned for its three kilometre long lagoon and strong winds which funnel through a gap in the ridge onto the beach. World windsurf and kite championships are held here every year, but the well equipped centre provides courses and equipment for all levels of experience, and the beach has lifeguards in attendance every day.

In the north of the island the shallow shelving beaches at Corralejo beneath the sand dunes are also popular with wind surfers and kite riders.

Fishing

Beach and deep water fishing is very popular in the island. Casting off the beaches and rocky coastline fishermen regularly catch barracuda and sea bass, and local people, using live crabs as bait often bring in fine parrot fish known locally as La Vieja. The deep waters off the island are a favourite amongst game fishermen, with big marlin, swordfish, tuna, bonito and wahoo being landed during the game fishing season which runs from April to November. Fishing trips from boats can be arranged at most of the marinas along the east coast.

Walking

Walking is growing in popularity throughout the island, and a series of marked paths are now being planned, which will enable walkers to trek from one end of the island to other a week long walk of more than 155 kms (100 miles). The plains and hills are crisscrossed with ancient paths, so best walk with a guide if possible. There are several walking companies which offer guided walks through some of the most beautiful parts of the islands, from the dunes of Corralejo to the rugged high volcanic cliffs above the wild and beautiful Cofete beach in the south. In the middle of the island a popular trek takes walkers through the old historic town of Betancuria the first European settlement in the Atlantic along a green valley watered by distinctive windmills of the 1930s introduced to the island by returning immigrants from the USA. Close by, in the pretty village of Vega de Río de Palmas, a path leads to a rocky ravine where the tiny chapel to the Virgen de la Peña is perched on the side of a rocky ravine.

Her saint's day in September is celebrated with a Romeria or procession which draws islanders from all over Fuerteventura. Other walks in the south take trekkers up from the beach of Cofete to the lofty mist shrouded peak of Mount Jandia, at 807 metres the highest on the island. The historic volcanic core of Tindaya near La Oliva has excellent views to Lanazarote, and sometimes even Mount Teide on distant Tenerife. Here, the distinctive podomorphs foot-shaped carvings left by the original settlers on the island more than a thousand years ago can be found on the summit. Walkers must have a permission from the Environmental Agency (Medio Ambiente) and have to be accompanied by a park guard.

Cycling

With good empty roads, guaranteed sunshine and few steep gradients , cycling is a poplar activity for visitors and islanders alike. Bikes can be hired from the major centres in Morro Jable, and Corralejo, and recently opened dedicated cycle and mountain bike tracks lead to most of the island's most spectacular locations. Cycle hire companies usually arrange day rides, taking riders to interior locations for downhill rides to the coast. Most rides end on the beach, or follow the coast so that cyclists can always have a cooling dip during the day. A very popular 25 kilometre ride runs from Corralejo to Cotillo on a dedicated cycle track above by rocky coves and deserted beaches on of the most beautiful parts of the northern coast.

Horse riding

A stable near the central village of Triquivajate offers riding on the island and caters for beginners and more experienced riders. With wide open unfenced terrain and little or no traffic to be encountered on the inland country tracks and roads, conditions are ideal. Once a month riders go out for 6 hour rides across the rocky plains by the light of the full moon.

Nature & Wildlife in Fuerteventura

Fuerteventura was granted the status of a Biosphere Reserve by UNESCO in May 2009 in recognition of its extraordinarily rich and unique natural setting. The Biosphere Reserves are large scale studies for demonstrating sustainable development on a regional scale and it is hoped that the award will secure the island's future as a high quality sustainable tourism destination. Of the total coastline of 326 km (202 miles), the eastern coast of low cliffs, long beaches and sand dunes has wetlands and sand dunes with many endemic and rare species of plants and birds.

The western coast, with over one hundred kilometres of cliffs and beaches are virtually untouched by man, making it unique in the Canary Island archipelago. The interior, with the largest area of extensive dry steppe in the entire Canary Islands, provides habitats for rare birds - like the Houbara Bustard, Egyptian Vulture and the endemic Canary Islands Chat, a tiny black headed sparrow-like bird once found in all the islands but now only on Fuerteventura.

All mammals on the island have been introduced accidentally - or as in the case of the camel, donkey and goat - deliberately. Shepherds and their flocks of goats are a common sight in the hills and on the rolling plains; the goat meat and milk of Fuerteventura is reckoned to be the best of the Canaries for the animals feed on the wild grasses, lichens and aromatic herbs which grow wild on the dry steppe and scree. Feral donkeys and goats roam freely in some of the more remote parts of the island on the west coast

There are thirteen natural protected parks and areas on the island which means that nearly 50 percent of the total land area is under legal protection or has conservation status. Plans are afoot to create a National Park along the west coast, an area of more than 100 kilometres in length which would include beaches once used by loggerhead and leatherback turtles to lay eggs.

The Environmental Agency of Fuerteventura has launched an ambitious project to reintroduce turtles to the west coast, and now loggerhead turtle eggs are being brought each year from the Cape Verde Islands to the beach of Cofete, where they are placed in artificial nests on the beach. The vulnerable hatchlings which emerge are then kept in special tanks for about two years before being released. In ten years or so it is hoped that for the first time in a century female loggerheads will return to the beaches to lay their eggs once more

The island of Fuerteventura rises sheer from the sea bottom which is nearly 1 kilometre (0.6 mile) deep just off the coast, and the upwelling of nutrient rich currents here attract fish of all kinds. Sperm and blue whales are often seen close to the coast, and pods of resident dolphins and pilot whales are frequent visitors to inshore waters on both sides of the island. The protected nature park of the Isla de los Lobos has areas of marine wetlands which are vital stopover for birds on the western migration route from Africa to Europe.

Now for the first time some species are nesting on the island avoiding the long hazardous flight to northern Europe and Siberia - an indication that the island is becoming safer for birds and perhaps that climate change is also disturbing long established patterns. There are plans to reintroduce here the Mediterranean monk seal, one of Europe's most endangered species. The seal colony here was hunted to extinction by pirates who used the island as a base to attack ships returning to Europe from the New World.

Geologically the island is a treasure house of information. Its rugged rock formations reveal the creation of the islands from the first eruptions to the most recent. With practically no trees or vegetation the rock structures are easily visible and with 50 sites of registered paleontological interest researchers are gaining invaluable insights into climatic changes and formation of volcanic oceanic islands.

Nightlife

Fuerteventura nightlife is relatively low key, compared to the other Canary Islands and resorts on mainland Spain. There are nightclubs and bars to meet the needs of tourists and locals, but it hasn't got a reputation for attracting large groups of late teenagers and twenties. The resorts of Corralejo, Caleta de Fuste and Jandia have the most night life aimed at tourists, and the capital of Puerto del Rosario has its own clubs and bars to attract local people.

There is one Casino on the island in Caleta de Fuste at the Carlota Hotel, which has all the usual features of a large casino and is open until 5am in the summer months and 4am in the winter months.

Fuerteventura nightlife in the resort's bars is based on entertainment which seems to be aimed at English speakers, with UK sports being shown on TV, vocalists, karaoke, quizzes, race nights and other shows.

The hotels have their own nightly entertainment programmes, which usually start with a children's disco at 8.30pm, followed by a show. These shows can be with professional artists or feature the hotel's entertainment team, and it is common to see adapted shows of Grease, Les Miserables, Starlight Express etc. They usually operate on a 2 weekly cycle of shows, so that anyone who stays for 14 days doesn't see the same show twice.

Many people who are self catering, go out in the evening to local restaurants and bars, as there is so much choice available. Other people make the most of the good climate and have BBQ's at their rented apartment or villa.

All bars and restaurants are child friendly, so it is acceptable to take children with you when enjoying nightlife, and they will offer child menus, a range of drinks and ice cream. Many bars are open until late, and some have licenses to open until the early hours.

If you want to party like the locals, it would be a good idea to find out when one of the town or village fiestas is taking place, and this will be a special type of Fuerteventura nightlife. They have traditional evening entertainment, and the local bands and groups will play and sing through to around 5am. It's very similar during the Carnival events during February and March.

Fuerteventura Nightlife in the main resorts

- In Corralejo, the main nightlife is based in and around the old town, where there are many bars and restaurants where late night open-air dining and drinking is popular. The Atlantico Center has a range of bars and clubs which are open until the early hours, as is the Waikiki Beach Bar next to the beach. Popular late night venues are Flicks Bar, Rock Island Bar, Caspers Lounge Bar, Blue Rock and The Talk Of The Town.

- In Caleta de Fuste, the bars and restaurants are in the small commercial centres such as the Castillo Centro, C.C. El Castillo and Los Arcos, and there are a few late night venues such as Aloha Gardens, Alhambra, Pieros Music Cafe, Hemmingways and Legends 60's Bar.

- In Jandia the nightlife is centered in the commercial area fronting the promenade, with the Centro Commercial de Jandia being the focal point.

So there is plenty of Fuerteventura nightlife, but it is more limited than on the other Canary Islands. But what can beat eating al fresco late at night, followed by drinks in an ideal climate, all the year round? You may then want to go to a late night club or return to your hotel, apartment or villa. I'm sure that you'll always remember your holiday nights.

Things to Do: Activities and Attractions

The American Star has now sunk into history

The SS America was launched by Eleanor Roosevelt on August 31, 1939, However, due to World War II, the inaugural trip was cancelled and the ship was drafted into war service. It was sucessful in evacuating around 483,000 soldiers.

After the war, the ship was returned to its owners and restored to its original luxurious condition and on December 14, 1946 she made her true maiden voyage. From 1946 to 1964 the ship crossed the Atlantic Ocean man times, until commercial aircraft flights began to displace cruise ships. In 1964, it was decommissioned.

A Greek shipping company acquired her in October 1964 and renamed her the SS Australis. She was modernized, and put into service to transport imigrants and tourists. In this new stage, she had a capacity for 2,300 passengers. She was then later sold and renamed again but due to lack of maintenance and her age she became unusable.

In 1993 she was bought by a Thai ship owner for two million dollars with plans to convert her into floating luxury hotel in Bangkok and she was again renamed the American She was to be taken there in tow by a Ukrainian tugboat.

During a major storm on January 15, 1994 in the Canary Islands the tugboat had to cut the towing cable and the American Star drifted towards Playa Garcey, and was broken in two by the strength of the conditions.

In July that year it was declared a total loss and the ship became the victim of looting by locals. Many of the fixtures and fittings ended up in a a bar in Puerto del Rosario named the Naufragio (shipwreck). The wreck then became a real attraction despite the difficulty in getting to the beach. People have swept out to sea and drowned in an attempt to get to the ship, as although it looked close to shore the currents there can be very strong.

After spliting in two, the stern sank into the ocean. The forward half, remained and was known as a ghost ship. There is now nothing left of the wreck.

Beaches

The Beaches of Fuerteventura

A page seems hardly sufficient to cover the beaches of Fuerteventura, after all there are around 125 miles of beach on the island. In time this page may become two or three or even more, but to be going on with here is a summary of some of the magnificent beaches to be found here on Sunny Fuerteventura. Naturism, or nudism is acceptable all over Fuerteventura, but with so much beach available they tend to use the quieter stretches of beach away from the general family holidaymakers.

If you have a favourite beach you would like us to mention, we will be more than happy to go and road test it.

Costa Calma
This beach is part of the Playa de Sotavento (Leeward beach) de Jandia. It is a long wide beach with a narrow band of scrubland between the beach and the rise where the buildings begin. This area is popular with naturists. The beach is cleaned daily to remove weed that washes up there. The sea is pleasant for swimming and there are a couple of sanitary blocks on the beach itself. Naturists in this area tend to frequent the area where there are some shrubs, for privacy.

Corralejo Grandes Playas
The beaches to the south of Corralejo, along the east coast, are situated in the Parque Natural de Corralejo. Those between Corralejo and the two large hotels are used for umpteen things. From beach to beach the conditions vary and sports enthusiasts use them for surfing, windsurfing and kiteboarding. Naturists use the quieter parts of the

beach about 200 metres either side of the large hotels. There are some large circular rock constructions that can give shelter or privacy. When the tide is out there are rockpools and small waders come in to feed. The bus between Corralejo and the hotels runs every 30 minutes in either direction, and a walk along the beach is a lovely way to pass a couple of hours; more if you like to stay a while.

Corralejo
Corralejo is at the northern tip of the island and is built around what was originally a small fishing port. There are several beaches in the immediate area. The ones closest to the town centre are family friendly as they provide a safe environment, and they are also close to the facilities that a family may need. A family beach with no naturists.

Caleta De Fuste / Costa Caleta
Caleta De Fuste is a purpose built resort. It is based around the large horseshoe shaped cove. The natural features of this cove, or caleta, mean that there is a gentle slope into the sea, it is protected from waves, and there are no dangerous currents. The beach is currently being upgraded, which will make it much larger. The work should be completed by the end of February 2017.

Sotavento
Sotavento beach is quite different in nature depending on whether the tide is in or out. When it is out it is a an expansive beach where you

tend to be sand-blasted. When it is in the beach disappears to be replaced by a spit that runs for a couple of kilometeres.

Playa Blanca, Puerto Del Rosario
Playa Blanca is a short walk from the centre of Puerto del Roasario. The white sand stretches for about half a mile and at the far end of the beach there is a warning sign about the nature of the currents, however during the summer ther is a flag system to show when it is safe to bathe. There are also lifeguards there at busy periods. It is used by the locals when they fancy an hour at the beach and by surfers as there is usually some surf there. There is very little topless bathing, so naturism is probably not acceptable here.

This beach had a **facelift** to extend and improve the beach in 2007 and now has Blue Flag status.

El Cotillo Beach
The white sandy beaches stretch for miles to the south of El Cotillo. They are on the west coast of the island and therefore the waves tend to be larger than average. The size of the beaches means that even on a busy day it is possible to have lots of space to yourself. You can get the number seven bus from Puerto Del Rosario, or the number eight from Corralejo. The beach to the south of El Cotillo is huge and so it is easy to find a quiet spot for naturist bathing.

A popular spot for visitors to El Cotillo are the lagoons which are on the road north of the village towards the lighthouse, and along the shoreline to the east of the lighthouse. White sand and clear blue shallow water are an attractive feature alongside the volcanic rock.

Jandia

The beach at Morro Jable is also known as the Playa del Matorral, and also as Playas de Jandia. The beach has the usual water sports activities going on and it is possible to go sailing in a hired boat. The beach at Jandia is informally divided into a naturist section to the left of the lighthouse when looking out to sea, and a clothed, but not many, to the right. There are sunbeds available on both sections and the sea is pleasant for swimming. Morro Jable's naturists tend to frequent the area to the left of the Lighthouse as you are looking towards the sea.

Cofete

The beach at Cofete is a white sandy beach that is about 5km in length. It is not easily reached and this means that there is plenty of room to get away from other people, if you wish to do so. We found the surf to be a bit on the rough side and would recommend taking great care if bathing. As the beach is huge there is plenty of room for naturists.

Ajuy

Ajuy has a long black sandy beach, where you can see some interesting geological features. There is a nice walk along the cliffs to a cave and a viewpoint looking out to the sea. The restaurant on the beach and those close by are Spanish owned. The day we went there we didn't do any bathing and we didn't see anyone else bathing either so we are not sure what the water is like.

Lobos Island
A trip to the Island of Lobos will give you access to a beautiful sandy beach which has a gentle slope into the water. We can recommend this for bathing and there are plenty of fish to be seen if you fancy trying snorkelling.

Playa Chica, Puerto del Rosario
Playa Chica beach in Puerto has recently had some work done to enlarge it. Its now a lovely beach which is popular at weekends with the Spanish.

Fuerteventura Fishing
Fuerteventura has a very long coastline and an abundance of fish around its shores. This makes it an ideal place for angling, whether it be a serious attempt to catch a whopper like the one on the photo, which weighs in at 200kg, or a relaxing couple of hours of amusement.

All the game fish shown below are primarily caught with artificial fish, shallow & deep diving plugs, the Yo-Zuri magnetic series plugs are very popular with the locals in Caleta de Fuste, which is why Gone Fishing, the tackle shop in Caleta de Fuste started stocking them

The three photos show 4 bonita tuna (Sarda sarda) and a barracuda, a bluefish and a brace of Garfish. They were all caught fishing from the rocks in the Caleta de Fuste area of Fuerteventura.

They can also be caught using jigs (soft body rubber fish) or spinners (conventional or specialized new ones such as metalic sardines & artificial minnows, or a combination of spinner & rubber fish in one lure). Success rate is also good with live bait (boga) or dead bait (sardine). Boga is caught relatively easily by fishing with a variety of baits & methods (jigging with small pieces of squid or float fishing with small treble hooks & paste).

Crab is the best bait when fishing for Parrotfish. Squid and prawns are the number one bait for all other species (bottom feeders such as the Breams, Snappers, Blacktail Combers, Rays, Small Sharks, Angel Fish, Scorpion Fish, etc).

Bread paste works with some species, but is better if it's mixed with other stuff, such as smelly cheese, sardines or oily extracts. However, it comes off the hooks very easily and can be very frustrating!!

The greedy lizard fish can be caught on just about any of the above mentioned baits. When Aram of Gone Fishing caught this 8" long one it was trying to swallow a 5" wrasse that he was bringing in. It was nowhere near the hook but half the wrasse was in its mouth and its teeth are so sharp & slanted inwards, there was no way that the wrasse was coming out of its mouth without a little help

Fishing on your Fuerteventura holiday.

If your interest lies in knocking out a few small fish to while away a sunny afternoon there is ample scope to do so while on sunny Fuerteventura.

The paste used to catch these small fish, an angel fish and an ornate wrasse, is a mixture of bread, flour, tuna and egg yoke. The exact quantities may be important, but just bunging the ingredients together will produce results. As the paste tends to drop of the hook rather easily, the locals use three or four single hooks on short leads of the same length. The paste is attached to the hooks and plonked into the water. Having several hooks helps keep the bait on and increases the chances of a bite resulting in a fish.

Fly fishing on Fuerteventura?? This gentleman is a keen fly fisherman and brought his gear with him on holiday.

He spent the week creating flies and fishing off the rocks around Caleta de Fuste. Some of the flies were made to look like bread crust, and some success was had. Nothing enormous, but he enjoyed being able to practise his favourite form of fishing while here on Fuerteventura.

Some fish here need to be handled with care. These include the Scorpion fish. The spines carry a poison that will result in a painful swelling if you are unlucky enough to have sufficient contact with them. The best policy might be to avoid touching them, and they genearlly advertise their poisonous nature by having bright colours.

If, like Steve from Pembrokeshire, you know what you are doing, there is a greater range of options available to you, but even absolute beginners such as William, from Brackley, with a little help from dad Terry, show that fishing in Fuerteventura can be fun. William is a lot less likely to catch the sun, and Steve was catching a few rays around Christmass. It wouldn't be wise to do so in the summer as a couple of hours in the sun here would result in sunburn

Home Making on Sunny Fuerteventura.

So, you have finally taken the plunge and bought a property in Fuerteventura, and now you need to go about turning it into a home.

Following the links on this page will lead you to a page that tells you about the named sponsor.

Kitchens

When you buy a newly built house on Sunny Fuerteventura, it is often the case that a kitchen will not have been included in the purchase price.

Living Rooms

There is the usual range of furniture shops to be found on the island, ranging from small outlets that cater for those that like to feel that their furnishings are individual to hypermarkets that supply furniture for every part of the house.

Bathroom

Your bathroom in Fuerteventura will probably get more use than the one you had in your home country, as it is very refreshing to have a shower, particularly during periods of hot weather. Many bathrooms have no bath as such, but for those of you that like to wallow it is possible to have a bathroom designed and built to meet your own needs.

Pools and Jacuzzi.

Though many homes are situated on complexes that have communal pools it is possible to splash out and have your own pool or jacuzzi fitted. There are companies that will arrange to have a spa fitted as an integral part of you garden design.

If you are in the business of home improvement, and wish to be involved with a quality website please contact us using the link below or 'phoning us 647 819 397

Air Conditioning.

Air conditioning allows you to enjoy the cool interior of your home, even if the temperatures outside are approaching 40 degrees, and having the air in your home cooled by a professionally fitted air conditioning unit also reduces the humidity inside your living space.

Shopping on Fuerteventura

Fuerteventura has a full range of shops, catering for the needs of those that live here as well as those that only visit from time to time.

One of the interesting features of the shops on Fuerteventura, is that they are sometimes designed in a way to cope with the climatic conditions. As it is often windy, and can sometimes be quite dusty, many of the shopping centres have unexpectedly small entrances. You can often enter a small doorway and find yourself in a large shopping centre.

Puerto del Rosario

The two main shopping streets in Puerto del Rosario are Leon y Castillo and Avd Juan de Betancourt. See the Puerto del Rosario map. Having said this it is worth a wander round Puerto as there are some interesting shops tucked away down the side streets. You need to bear in mind that the shops in Puerto tend to stick to the siesta closing times, being open in the morning and again in the late afternoon. The biggest shopping centre there is Las Rotundas, with many big name shops. There is now a Lidl supermarket opposite the Risco Prieto just outside Puerto.

Corralejo

There are lots of shops on the main street of Corralejo, and a few new shopping centres have opened there. As is the case with the other resorts, more shops tend to be located in the commercial centres that are dotted around the town. See the Corralejo map for the locations of some of the commercial centres. We are still developing this map. A recent shopping centre to open is Las Campanario

Caleta de Fuste

Besides the Atlantico Shopping Centre, where you might pop into on of the bars and restaurants there for refreshments, there are several smaller commercial centres dotted around the town. The shops include various jewellers and perfume shops, as well as gift shops, clothing retailers and electrical retailers. Caleta has a market each Saturday morning by the bus station.

Morro Jable

There are lots of shops along the main street in Morro Jable that cater for the needs of tourists. These are set back under a shaded walkway, and are a good option for getting out of the sun for a while. There are also a couple of commercial centres just off the main street. The old part of Morro Jable is much more congested, but has lots of shops that cater for the needs of residents.

Markets.

There are markets held in Corralejo, (Mondays and Fridays at the Baku waterpark). Caleta de Fuste (Saturday mornings) Jandia (Thursday) and Costa Calma (Sunday). All offer an interesting alternative to the shops.

Supermarkets

There are several supermarket chains that hav stores in Fuerteventura. The Netto chain is most prominent in the tourist area, and is related in some way to the Hiperdino stores, which are to be found away from the tourist areas and are generally cheaper. The Spar stores in Corralejo and the Atlantico Centre are used by tourists and locals and the Inspecasa chain have stores dotted around the island, including some in relatively small villages such as El mattoral and

Lajares. The supermarkets in Caleta used to be quite expensive, but I find that at the moment the prices are quite reasonable.

Touring on Fuerteventura.

Fuerteventura offers lots of scope for day trips by car, bus or even walking. It is well worth going out to visit different places as each part of the island differs so much.

When we did the trips, we were working. A tough job but somebody has to do it! With a little planning, most of the trips can be converted into a relaxing day out, and you can take time to explore all the variety and beauty Fuerteventura has to offer. The obvious attractions are the 125 different Fuerteventura beaches, such as those in Jandia, to the smaller more interesting beaches such as the one by the caves ofAjuy

Hiring a car.

It is easy to drive in Fuerteventura as the roads are laid out to make it simple, even when you are only used to driving on the left! Altough the islands are getting busier the roads are usually clear. They are in the process of completing new motorways too. Getting to the more secluded beaches involves driving down tracks., It is probably best to hire a four wheel drive vehicle, although we did these tours by car. If using a hire car, you may not be insured off road, so it's best to check the terms and conditions of your car hire company.

Touring by bus.

The buses here are very reliable and there are about 16 different bus routes on the island. Traveling on the bus is quite cheap and you can get tickets that give 10% discount. We have found the bus drivers to be friendly, and the cost of fares is usually on the side of the door as you enter the bus. See the Getting about page for details. The bus timetables are on the right.

Walking on Fuerteventura

Waking on Fuerteventura is a much more enjoable pastime outside of the summer months, because although the weather in Fuerteventura does not vary a great deal throughout the year, it is warmer and much sunnier in the height of summer, and if you walk any distance you will need to carry plenty of fluids, and make sure you are protected from the sun.

The local government bodies in Fuerteventura have invested a lot of money into creating coastal walkways, such as the one that runs between Caleta de Fuste and Costa Antigua, where you can stop to feed the chipmonks, and these provide a way of going for a short stroll in whatever footwear you choose to wear, but for the more serious walks it is necessary to have some suitable shoes or boots. It rarely rains, but in the winter months the wind can be quite cool, especially in the mountains, so at least one additional layer of warm clothing is a good idea.

The landscape on Fuerteventura tends to resemble a mars scape, especially in the summer when the mountains become redder as the rocks warm up. The landscape is the result of millions of years of weathering of a remains of the volcanoes that formed Fuerteventura.

Ferries to the Lobos Island from Corralejo, and it is possible to walk around the entire island, including going up to the peak of the caldera, wich provides excellent views of Fuertentura and Lanzarote. As Lobos is a nature reserve, walkers are asked to stick to the tracks, and it has been suggested that the climb to the top of the Caldera should be closed. The photograph on the right is a view of Puerto del Rosario from near Costa Antigua. The walk from Caleta de Fuste to Puerto del Rosario along the coast covers about 8 miles, with the majority of the walk being along tracks

Over the past couple of years the Cabildo of Fuerteventura (the Island's Council) have spent money on reinstating a network of footpaths (red Canaria de Senderos) all over the island.

The footpaths have signposts and information (in Spanish, English and German) boards. The information is detailed with maps, level of difficulty, time, terrain and interesting things to look out for. Unfortunately the Cabildo have not yet published a map of these routes.

Some routes are:

Vega de Rio Palma to Toto

Vega de Rio Palma to Ajuy

Casillas de Morales to Caldera de Gayria

Valles de Santa Iñes to Betancuria

Betancuria to Vega de Rio Palma

Antigua to Betancuria

Triquivijate to Barranco La Amuley

Triquivijiate to Rosa del Taro

Fuerteventura sailing

Although Fuerteventura has the ideal conditions for it, sailing is less popular than for example kitesurfing and windsurfing. The reason for that could be the fact that, although there are several harbours on Fuerteventura, there are only a few sheltered bays where you can drop anchor and dropping anchor at an idyllic spot is what most of the people that are travelling with large yachts are looking for.

On the island there are several Escualas Nauticas, sailing schools, where the local children and adults can learn how to sail and surf. In the afternoon and early evening you can see, in for example Puerto de Rosario, the pupils in their 420 and 470 dingys sailing in and at close range of the harbour.

The usual type of boat that you will see most here is not the 420 or the 470, but the catamaran, which you can rent in several places on Fuerteventura. If you want to rent a sailing boat you should remember to take your sailing certificate with you. The last to mention are the yachts. You can frequently see them sail by a few hundred metres from the east coast of Fuerteventura. They are usually part of a group of yachts of the same type that sail together from one island to the other. Because the winds are often strong and the crew maybe not that experienced, they often only sail on the foresail, and you can´t blame them really, because it´s not very comfortable when your floating home lies under an angle of 45 degrees when you try to cook or get other things done below deck

On the Canaries they have their own traditional boats, the Vela Latinas, which are also used in regattas. They were originally designed as fishing boats with latin rigging a fixed keel and a crew of up to five people. If you want to see these boats you can go to the harbours of Puerto del Rosario and Corralejo.

As mentioned earlier you can rent out the small catamarans, but if you like to treat yourself to some time on a really big and expensive boat, then you can book a trip on one of the catamarans which provide 4 to 5 hour trip. These trips are usually fully catered, with food and drinks are included in the price. If you are lucky you may encounter dolphins, turtles or flying fish on your journey.

For a slightly different take on sailing, have a look at our Los Achipencos page. If you are here when this event is on its well worth a visit.

Scuba Diving, Fuerteventura

If you are considering coming to the Canary Islands for a diving holiday you should bear in mind that With its crystal clear waters and consistent water temperatures, Fuerteventura is a divers' paradise. The water temperature around the Canary Islands ranges from 18 to 22 degrees, and this range of temperatures is ideal for supporting the multi-organism ecosystem that exists around Fuerteventura's coast.

Fuerteventura Dive Centres

There are about a dozen dive centers, around the coast of Fuerteventura. They all run courses for divers with various levels of ability, and a day spent taking part on a taster course makes for a very enjoyable day out. You are guaranteed to see a wide range of species. Diving in the Canaries is like taking a dip in your own zillion litre fish tank, and Fuerteventura offers some of the best diving in the Canary islands.

Given that you are fit enough to dive, and that your time of your dive will leave sufficient time before you fly home, a typical beginners course will pan out in the following way. The first part of the course will include a theory lesson to teach you the basic theory including safety procedures, how the equipment works and the hand signals you can expect to use. You will then have a practice session in a pool to allow you to become accustomed to the equipment and allow the staff to correct your dive weights if they need to. Then it is off to the sea for a dive that lasts about thirty minutes. You will need to be careful because once you have had a taste in the shallows, you may become hooked and filled with a desire to head further out into the deep blue ocean.

Snorkelling in Fuerteventura

There is lots of fun to be had snorkelling in the clear water off the wonderful beaches of Fuerteventura.

Fish and other marine life tend to congregate around rocks, so you wil need to swim along and look in the nooks and crannies.

As the water is so clear, you don't have to dive beneath the water if you don't want to. There will be many things that you can see if you look in the right places.

One of my favourite spots is La Lajita beach, not the main beach but one to the right. Here there are lots of rocks close to the beach and there is lots to see. It can be difficult to get out of the water though if the sea is rough!

Corralejo also is good for snorkelling as again there are rocks just off the beach.

I think the best place in Caleta is by the Atlantico centre.

Fuerteventura surfing

In the eighties Fuerteventura was discovered as a surfers' paradise. That's why Fuerteventura is also called the "European Hawaii".

The best surfspots can be found in the northern part of the island between Corralejo and El Cotillo. There you can surf the so called

"Reefbreaks", where the waves break on the rocks. Other kinds of waves you can surf are "Beachbrakes".

Another well known surfspot can be found to the south of El Cotillo. Because the best northern surfspots can only be reached through dustroads it is recommended to use a four-by-four to avoid damaging your (hired) car. You should also bring enough food and drinks with you because you won't find any shops or restaurants there.

Those who want to learn to surf could rent a board, just start trying, but it's better to take at least a few surfing lessons. With the instructions of an experienced surfing teacher you will learn a lot faster than when you try to find out everything on your own, and besides he will know the best surfspots and can give you inside information on, for example, dangerous currents. There are one day courses but you can also sign up for a surfcamp where you get several days of surfing lessons. You are provided with a board and a wetsuit, taken to and from the surfspots and it's usually fully catered. The paddling through the waves is physically demanding so you should be reasonably fit. So exercise and swim a little bit before you take surfing lessons!

Briefly, the theoretics of surfing are like this. First you have to get behind the breaking waves. To do that you can take the board sideways and push it throught the waves. But when the water gets deeper you will have to lay yourself on the board and start paddling. If you've managed to get behind the breaking waves you can try to catch a wave. For beginners the waves that have already broken, the white water waves, are the best ones to surf because all the powers of the wave are released in them and therefore it's easier to ride.

When you want to ride a wave that didn't break yet you will have to paddle first to catch some speed. After you've got enough speed, you should try stand up on the board. That should be done quickly and in one fluent movement. But make sure you choose the right position on the board. When you are standing too close to the top of the board it could dive, and when you are too far on the back end you will fall off the board. But if you jump up quick and on the right place on the board you might surf the whole wave until you reach the shore. On paper it looks easy, but it's actually very difficult and you will need a lot of practise!

At first you'll spend a lot more time in the water than on the board. But don't let this put you off. Because riding a wave is a great feeling and a few good rides will make up for all the effort.

Windsurfing on Fuerteventura

Windsurfing is a popular pastime all around the island of Fuerteventura. There are many locations around the island that you can use, each with its own pros and cons, depending on whether you are a beginner, or practising for the world championships. These held on Fuerteventura each year in Sotovento, in Jandia.

Beginners.

There are many places where you can learn to windsurf on the island, and several different operators provide lesson or courses. There are often trainee windsurfers in the cove at Caleta de Fuste. They are easy to spot because to begin with they have no sail! Then they get a small one, then a large one and then disappear off to somewhere that is more challenging.

More experienced

For those more experienced, there are many locations, some of them such as Corralejo bay, are easily accessed. The views of over to Lobos and Lanzarote from Corralejo are superb. The western side of the island tends to have stronger waves and the currents are stronger, so this side of the island is not really suitable for beginners.

World Champions

The world championships are held in Sotovento, in Jandia each year, and have been held there for about 20 years

If you have windsurfed at any location on the island, we would be more than happy to include your personal perspective within these pages.

We hope that the photographs taken at different locations will give you some idea of what to expect there.

Fuerteventura Kiteboarding

For over 30 years the world's best board sportsmen have battled annually for the World Championship off the coast of Fuerteventura due to the consistent wind and sunny weather. The event is generally held around July or August and the best windsurfers and kiteboarders will compete in the World Championship heats in three disciplines, Freestyle World Cup, Windsurfing Slalom World Cup and the Kitesurfing Strapless Freestyle Grand Slam.

After Fuerteventura was discovered in the eighties as a surfers paradise, the kitesurfers quickly followed. A lot of kitesurfers from the northern part of Europe used the opportunity to practise their sport as the flight time is only about four hours to strong winds, big waves, high temperatures and a lot of sun. Ideal conditions to practise all kinds of watersports. You can see the colourful kites as you approach the kitesurfbeaches near Corralejo and the Jandia coast.

Especially appealing to kitesurfers are the beaches of Jandia. The winds are very strong there because they are forced through the hills and are therefore enhanced. This phenomenon is also called the Sotavento Jet and occurs mainly in summer. This is the reason why since 1986, the International World Cups in Windsurfing (Freestyle, Speed and Slalom) and since 2001 also the freestyle, boardercross, hangtime, best tricks and kitespeed World Cup take place. Speeds of over 80 km/h can be reached! The hangtime (the time that board and rider are in the air) record is 8,87 seconds and was set here on Fuerteventura.

The Sotavento Jet is best left to the more experiences kiteboarder. To kitesurf there you should already have some experience and, for example, be able to sail up the wind because otherwise the prevailing northeast passat (tradewind) will take you out to open sea without you being able to reach the shore again! Beginners might, therefore, prefer to go to the beaches south of Corralejo or the lagoons near the dunes of Jandia (Risco del Paso). The wind overthere is a little bit less strong and in the lagoons of Jandia the water is only shallow which makes it easy to step on the board. Both the beaches of Jandia as the beaches near Corralejo have a special reserved watersport area. This to make sure there won´t be any collisions with other bathers.

Kitesurfing on the westcoast is only recommendable for experienced kitesurfers. Strong currents and high waves might be spectacular, but they can become dangerous for beginners. So just stick to spectating there if you are a beginner!

When you want to start kitesurfing it´s best to go to a kitesurfschool to get lessons, because kites can reach high speeds and you risk hurting yourself and others when you´re not able to keep your kite under control. There are kitesurfschool in Corralejo and in Jandia, where you can also rent kiteboards.

Birds on Fuerteventura

The birds on Fuerteventura are different to those that you would find back home. These photographs are of some of the birds I have seen since September 2004. For a birdwatching on Fuerteventura

These ptographs are of some of the birds that can be seen on Fuerteventura. It is possible to take passable photographs with a digital camera. Some were taken with a Nikon Coolpix 5000, and others with a Panasonic DMC-F27. The Nikon was not directly replaced and the Panasonic does have image stabilisation, which reduces camera shake problems.

This young Kestrel was in Morro Jable. I heard its parent making a fuss and took five or six pictures from about 30 feet. It is disappointing that they were slightly out of focus.

A great grey shrike. These are a common species on Fuerteventura. This one was singing away outside Cocosol.

Golf on Fuerteventura
A Guide to Fuerteventura's Golf Courses.

Fuerteventura Golf Course
Golf is a very popular sport on Fuerteventura. The first golf course on the Island was created in Caleta de Fuste (Costa Caleta). This is a really excellent course, designed by Juan Catarineu, and which hosted the Spanish Open in 2004, which was quite an achievement for a course which only opened in Spring 2002.

Despite Fuerteventura's almost constant sunshine and little rain, the golf course has beautiful greens. The winds provide a challenge for all golfers. there are three lakes and other natural hazards.

The golf course also boasts a 5 star clubhouse, the Elba Palace Golf Resort Hotel, which homes the pro shop and the resident PGA professional. It has a driving range, chipping area, practice bunker and putting green. Practice facilities include a 50 bay driving range, club and buggy hire, a large putting green and a second green for chipping and bunker shots.

This course is designed around luxurious villa complexes many of these villas being available for rental.

Las Salinas Golf Course.
The second course to open was built alongside the first one in Caleta. This is very well set up as a course that is ideal for the holidaymaker type golfer, as well as experienced golfer, it being slightly less challenging than Fuerteventura Golf Course. This course is currently maintained in very good condition.

It is a par 70 course designed for Manolo Piñeiro, twice world champion golfer. The course's amenities amenities include a club house, pro shop, buggy, trolley and club hire, a cafeteria, restaurant and changing rooms with showers and lockers.

Las Playitas Golf Course.
In 2010 the Golf course of Las Playitas opened the further nine holes required to make it a full golf course. There is a driving range, for around 30 golfers. It is a very well planned and challenging course.The pro here is British PGA professional Murdo McCorquodale, who speaks English, Spanish and German. The Golf Course at Las Playitas Golf course is just a few kilometres away fromGran Tarajal.

Corralejo Golf course.
There is a 9 hole course on the Parque Natural development in the south of Corralejo, and it´s called the Mirador de Lobos Golf. It´s a 673m course, with a practise net area and putting/chipping greens.

All in all Fuerteventura is developing into an ideal destination for those who like a little golf on holiday and for those that want an entire holiday designed around that theme.

Jandia Golf Course (Closed at the moment - Oct 2011).
The course in Jandia, on the right as you enter Morro Jable, though open still has a few teething problems. The course is quite hilly and would be more suitable if the course had buggiess, but at the moment there aren't any. The paths between tees aren't clearly defined and it can be difficult to find the next tee. It is well laid out and if the teething problems can be sorted out this promises to be a good course.

Thanks to Mr and Mrs Jones from arround Bicester for providing us with some information for this page. We met them at the Jandia Golf course and we were pleased that they were Sunnyfuerteventura.com fans.

Running in Fuerteventura

With its warm, dry climate, varying terrain and surfaces, Fuerteventura can offer runners a wide range of running experiences, whether you are a lifetime addict or fancy an occasional jog.

For those more challenging runs, we have a number of recommendations. Hill repetitions on Montagna Blanca give even the most hardened career runner a solid workout and once you have finished your last repetition, you can stop to take in the view over the golf course and beyond before your descent.

Speed repeats on the nearby "locals" beach of Playa Blanca offer a more sympathetic surface to work those legs and lungs! Once again you can always reward yourself. This time with a well earned breakfast on the beach while you "warm down" in the sun.

Tempo runs on the dirt tracks at the back of Fuerteventura airport are certainly a different holiday experience. With the sea on one side and aeroplanes landing on the other there is always something to look at whilst you cover a few kilometres. While John insists he can outrun a 737, he has yet to prove it!!!

But its not all about working hard. This is Fuerteventura, where taking it easy is the number one priority. For a more gentle running experience, the options are endless. John Polley has a number of regular routes in addition to those above.

When John was asked what he liked best about running on the island, he had this to say: "It's difficult to condense into a few words. I suppose my two favourite things are the weather (it hardly ever rains, it doesn't get freezing cold and you get proper daylight all day, all year round) and the numerous dirt tracks and unmade roads. In short a fantastic climate and plenty of off road tracks to explore new parts of the island that most people never see, even if they live here."

Further afield, there are a never ending supply of breathtaking experiences, in every sense of the word. The beach at Costa Calma offers kilometre after kilometre of flat compact golden sands, with an aquamarine ocean on one side and rocky cliffs and sand dunes on the other. A short drive will take you to any number of rocky hills and mountains, all with their own unique views and challenges. Every resort has its own set of beaches, hills, dirt tracks and curiosities to uncover.

Come out to the island and enjoy the running.

Walking on Fuerteventura

Waking on Fuerteventura is a much more enjoable pastime outside of the summer months, because although the weather in Fuerteventura does not vary a great deal throughout the year, it is warmer and much sunnier in the height of summer, and if you walk any distance you will need to carry plenty of fluids, and make sure you are protected from the sun.

The local government bodies in Fuerteventura have invested a lot of money into creating coastal walkways, such as the one that runs between Caleta de Fuste and Costa Antigua, where you can stop to feed the chipmonks, and these provide a way of going for a short stroll in whatever footwear you choose to wear, but for the more serious walks it is necessary to have some suitable shoes or boots. It rarely rains, but in the winter months the wind can be quite cool, especially in the mountains, so at least one additional layer of warm clothing is a good idea.

The landscape on Fuerteventura tends to resemble a mars scape, especially in the summer when the mountains become redder as the rocks warm up. The landscape is the result of millions of years of weathering of a remains of the volcanoes that formed Fuerteventura.

Ferries to the Lobos Island from Corralejo, and it is possible to walk around the entire island, including going up to the peak of the caldera, wich provides excellent views of Fuertentura and Lanzarote. As Lobos is a nature reserve, walkers are asked to stick to the tracks, and it has been suggested that the climb to the top of the Caldera should be closed. The photograph on the right is a view of Puerto del Rosario from near Costa Antigua. The walk from Caleta de Fuste to Puerto del Rosario along the coast covers about 8 miles, with the majority of the walk being along tracks.

Watersports on Fuerteventura.

Fuerteventura has a very long coastline in relation to its area. Nowhere is very far from the sea, which has a fairly constant temperature, and as the trade winds are a feature of life on Fuerteventura watersports are very popular.

Diving.
One of the main attractions of Fuerteventura for followers of all watersports is the fairly constant year round temperature of the water. The Canaries stream is responsible for the fairly constant sea temperature, and this results in an abundance of sea life, that makes diving such a pleasure.

Snorkelling
Snorkelling is a popular activity that is suitable for everyone. The clear pure waters around the island means that there is an abundance of sea life. There are snorkelling excursions that take you to the best sites.

Sailing

To go sailing you need wind and water (and a yacht!). Fuerteventura has an abundance of these. There are lots of harbours around the island and some offer sailing and fishing trips.

Surfing, Windsurfing and Kite boarding.
The strong surf around some parts of the island make Fuerteventura one of the best spots in the world for surfing. The reliable winds and a variety of water conditions mean that the needs of wind and kite surfers of any level of ability are catered for.

There is surf to suit all standards of surfer from the novice to the most experienced and adventurous surfer. Lessons are available for any of the disciplines at various centres around the island.

Cycling and mountain biking on Fuerteventura

The island of Fuerteventura offers a variety of opportunities for cyclists. Cycling around the larger tourist resorts is made easier by the presence of cycle paths. The asphalted roads, especially the newer ones, are generally of a good condition, and there are mile upon mile of new tracks that are a joy for those that like to get off-road on their mountain bikes.

Cycling events on Fuerteventura

Some cycling events have become part of the calendar on Fuerteventura. In February the Fuerte bike marathon takes place. The course is 86km long and the start and finish are in Corralejo. Photographs of 2005 Fuertebike mountain biking event with its quality international field of famous international mountain bikers can be seen at Fuertebike 2005

Another event that takes place in early December, again starting and finishing in Corralejo, is the Marcha Cicloturista. The original objective of the Marchas Cicloturistas, organised by the Instituto Canario de Investigación del Cáncer, ICIC, to raise awareness amomgst the population that sport plays an important role in keeping healthy and ppreventing the plague of obesity, which along with other illnesses results in a predisposition to contracting cancer. The event on Fuerteventura is also in memory of Pilar Cabrera, who in spite of having cancer worked tirelessly to promote awareness of the problem. The event involves cyclists following a 50km road route, with stops at Caldereta and La Olivia to allow the stragglers to catch up with those that treat the event as a race, and the professionals for whom the trip is a gentle stroll.

The event began in 2004, when some 400 cyclists took part. The event is always well organised and the participants are looked after. There is a bus for those that dont think they can make it ove the hilly section, and their bikes are taken in a lorry from the start of the second section to the Casa de Coronels, where the third stage begins.

Cycling on holiday

It is possible to make a holiday from touring the island. Roland and Ing, covered 600km in two weeks. There are plenty of hotels in Fuerteventura that are happy to provide accommodation for a couple of nights. On Wednesdays during the cruise season, you may see a peleton of cyclists in in Puerto del Rosario from the cruise ship Aida. The mountain bikes that the passengers use seem to be part of the equipment on board, and provide a means of seeing something of the area around the port whilst taking a little exercise

Achipencos, Fuerteventura

The Achipencos is a traditional part of the celebrations during carnival time in the capital of Fuerteventura, Puerto del Rosario. The locals turn out in force to see the valiant, and not so valiant, attempts to travel from the port area to a small beach just south of the port.

The vessels are each individually designed around a their own particular theme, and are powered by the efforts of the crew, with a little help, or hinderance from the wind.

The event is usually held on the first Sunday of Carnival Week, and the main road road alongside the port area is closed to traffic to make it safe for the thousands who turn out to watch. If there is inclement weather then it´s switched to the following Tuesday (Carnival Tuesday in Puerto and a local public holiday) or to the following Sunday.

The photographs that follow tell their own story. If you find yourself on the Island when this event is on, it makes for a fun day out.

Fuerteventura Feaga.

The feaga has been held on Fuerteventura for over 20 years, and is held by the side of the road to Pozo Negro. The Feaga is a VERY popular event here on the island. Judging by the number of cars going there at about 7pm on saturday evening, and the number of people there in the afternoon, you might be forgiven for thinking that if you did not attend you would have to pay a penalty of some sort.

The Feaga is a large agricultural show that grown to include a large number of displays, some of them more related to agriculture than others.

The goats are both rams. They are on very short tether and some were trying to butt their neighbours but couldn't reach. This one was staring at his neighbour in a very aggressive fashion.

Is the boy in the background impersonating the chicken?

The foal is a contender for the cutest thing at the show. There were about forty donkeys on display, as well as a couple of Shetland ponies and a mule or two.

As you can see the Feaga is well worth a visit, and we didn't even go for the evening's musical entertainment on the Saturday

Events and fiestas on Fuerteventura

Fuerteventura is often referred to as La Isla Tranquila, however we have found that there is always something happening on the island, with sporting events, market fairs, fiestas and general getting togetherness. Here you can find information and photographs on all the events we have covered so far.

For a list of forthcoming events , follow this link. If you know of anything we should add, please let us know.

Sporting events

There are lots of sporting events that happen throughout the year, and here is a summary:

CD Corralejo football team play their home games, every other weekend, at the Vincente Careno ground on the south side of the town. They play in the Spanish Third Division - Group 12 (Canary Islands). Admission is 5 euros for adults and free for children.

Motocross meetings are held at the Puerto del Rosario circuit and the Los Alares circuit (8km south of Caleta de Fuste) at various times during the year.

Car Rallies take place during the year, either on dirt track circuits or around the municipalities of the island. They are usually linked to the main Fiesta in the municipality ie in La Oliva, Puerto del Rosario, Antigua, Tuineje and Pajara.

There are cycling events that happen during the year including Fuerte-Bike (usually in February), an 85km mountain bike event that starts and finishes in Corralejo; Marcha Cicloturista (usually in December), a 50km cycle route that starts and finishes in Corralejo, which raises Cancer Awareness; and the Fundenas (usually at the end of October, over 2 days) which is a 188 km ride for around 800 cyclists from Corralejo to Morro Jable, with 90% of it being off-road.

A relatively new event is the Corralejo Dunes Half Marathon, held on the last weekend of October, with the majority of it being on the sand!

A weekend in March or April is the time for the Sports Fair, which is organised by the island council(Cabildo) and features most of the sports that are available on the island. It is very popular with locals and torists as it´s possible to try different sports and activities for free. It´s a fun atmosphere with the opportunity to try a range of sports from chess to bungee jumping!

Swimming events are also popular. In October there is the Bocaina Crossing, which is a 15 km swim from Playa Blanca on Lanzarote to Corralejo on Fuerteventura. On the same weekend is the 3.5 km swim the the Isla de Lobos to Corralejo.

Fiestas

There are Fiestas in all the towns and villages of Fuerteventura throughout the year. Each town or village has it´s local saint, and in the days leading up to the main saints day, there will be a variety of different events organised. These will include sporting events,traditional singing and dancing, and one or two all night open air dances which are called Verbenas. They start at around midnight and feature groups who perform throughout the night. On the actual Saints Day there will be a religious procession and Eucharist at the church. The last night will feature a firework display at around midnight. A Fiesta is a time to eat, drink and be merry!

We have covered some in Corrralejo and Puerto del Rosario, see the links for details.

Markets, Fairs and Celebrations

Besides the regular weekly markets thet are held at Corralejo, Caleta de Fuste, Costa Calma and Morro Jable, there are various fairs and other social gatherings, throughout the year.

The biggest island wide event is the Antigua Craft Fair (Feria de Artisana) which is held over the second weekend in May. Crafts people from the other Canary Islands and some from mainland Spain, have stalls at the Fair to demonstrate and sell their homemade goods. It´s attended by thousands of locals and visitors. It´s a free event.

Carnivals

During February and March it is the Carnival season on the island. Carnival events are held in Morro Jable, Gran Tarajal, Betancuria, Antigua, Caleta de Fuste, Puerto del Rosario and Corralejo.

Carnival events include singing and dancing competitions, local Murga groups singing satirical songs, Drag Queen Competitions, and any other event that is fun and unusual. In Puerto del Rosariothis includes a homemade car race and a raft race (Archipencos)from the Harbour to Playa Chica. Carnival events last several days, and usually on a Saturday evening, it is the Grand Carnival Parade. Hundreds of people dress in fancy dress through the towns, either as individuals or on floats or other vehicles. A parade is a colourful and noisey affair, where the food and drink flows! At the end of the Carnival there is a big firework display, and a traditional burning of a sardine.

Battle of Tamasite

The most important military events that have occurred in Tuineje, if not Fuerteventura, were the English attacks against Fuerteventura in 1740. These attacks stemmed from the Anglo-Spanish war, also known as the War of Jenkins' ear, which lasted from 1739 1742, before becoming part of the Austrian War of Succession. The war was characterised by a series of battles involving naval forces against varios ports and there were no clear gains on either side.

The war involved much privateering, a practice that involved a ship from one country being authorized to attack shipping of another country in return for a share of any booty. The targets of such raids regarded the perpetrators, with some degree of correcetness, as pirates, and the inhabitants of Fuerteventura still regard the attacks of 1740 as acts carried out by "English Pirates".

As a result of the Anglo-Spanish war the island was frequented by Corsairs who saw Fuerteventura as an easy target for the capture of civil ships, the booty from which could be sold in Madeira. During October and November of 1740 the ships, José Antonio, Fandango, The Star, San Augustine and Pedro Álvarez were captured and burned. On the 13th of October 1740, a contingent of troops from an English Corsair disembarked in the region of Gran Tarajal, and followed the gulley in the direction of Tuineje, where heavily armed, they performed looting and destruction, including to the town's church.

The lieutenant Colonel, Joseph Sánchez Umpiérrez, recruited people from the area and went in search of the English who were already retreating to their ship, and the two sides met in the Battle of El Cuchillete. The English consisted of 53 men with modern weapons and the Majoreros were armed with farming implements and used camels as shields. The lieutenant Colonel achieved a memorable victory in which 33 of the British died and the remainder were taken prisoner.

The other battle happened on the 24th of November when 55 soldiers disembarked at Gran Tarajal and again marched to Tuineje where looting and pillaging of the church occurred to an extent that greatly angered the Majeros, who had had strong religious sentiments. This time the natives knew of the disembarkation beforehand, and were able to assemble a larger force that was better armed as a result of having the weapons that they had captured the previous month. This force met the British in the Battle of Llano Florido, popularly know as the battle of Tamasite, and wiped them out.

The ferocity of the islander's was inflamed by the repetition of the destructive acts carried out by the British, including the destruction of the means of subsistence in the middle of a remote island. As result the fury of the Majoeros could not be tempered by their own leader, and this led to the complete destruction of the British force

XiX International Kite Festival, Festival International de Cometas , Playa del Burro

This festival gets bigger and better each year. This year the weather was very pleasant with the winds strong enough for the kite flying, but there was a calima on which spoiled the normal deep blue skies that backdrop the kites.

The event was popular and people passing by couldn't help but notice the brightly coloured kites, and many stopped to take a look and a walk around the beach.

The event opened at 9.30am on the Friday, and then and Saturday and Sunday there was a spectacular exhibition of acrobatic and static kites. At 10 am on Friday schoolchildren from the island arrived and under supervision they learned some of the tecniques used in kite flying, and had a chance to watch watch the best kiters in the world flying their kites.

Other events included this year a Kite Combat competition "Rokakus". And a kiting by night exhibition at the Las Cavellinas beach, which is near the Waikiki bar in Corralejo.

The kites were flown again on Sunday and there was a raffle in aid of charity. On Sunday evening the was a final meeting and then a closing ceremony at Playa Las Cavellinas.

A Fuerteventura Wedding, one couples Experience

The couple had been together quite a while, when they visited Caleta de Fuste together for the first time in 2001. They both loved the place and decided to buy a property here. When a proposal arrived out of the blue one day, she accepted and the wedding plans began. As a Register Office is not too romantic a venue, it was decided that they would get married in Fuerteventura.

Finding a venue

An initial enquiry to the Elba Sara Golf Hotel, revealed that it wasn't possible to hold the wedding ceremony there, however, the hotel on this occasion, would endeavour to help with the arrangements.an interpreter was found and the preparations began.

Obtaining documentation

To begin with, as they were both divorced, they had to take the divorce documents to the Register Office to get a certificate of no impediment, the certificate alone cost £120. The documents all had to be taken in person to the Foreign office in London to get the stamp of Hague Apostil. Next, in March a visit to the British Embassy at Las Palmas, to collect the Spanish Certificate of No Impediment was required, the trip was very quick within the hour they were back at Las Palmas airport for the Binter Canarias flight to Fuerteventura. The next day all the Spanish translation of documents were ready, and in person with the interpreter, visited the Court house in Puerto del Rosario to ensure that all the papers were correct. They both came out to Caleta de Fuste at Easter to file the papers at Jugazado de Puerto del Rosario and request the wedding date.

Setting the date

They asked for a certain date in August for the wedding as friends had already booked their flights and accommodation. After deciding that Antigua had a prettier venue for the ceremony, they then had to go to Ayuntamiento de Antigua to request the wedding file be transferred to there. Six weeks later they were given confirmation that the paperwork was in order and the wedding could go ahead. The date and venue were finally arranged August. at 5pm.

The wedding details

The rest of the wedding was sorted out in England, as the dresses, balloons, confetti, table plan and cards were all made in England. The flowers (roses) and photography including a video were arranged with people in Puerto del Rosario, the Rolls Royce was hired from the hotel, the Mercedes was loaned from a friend, and they hired a coach from Maxorata for the guests.

It is quite interesting getting the paperwork together, 3 trips to Fuerteventura, legal fees costing approximately £600.The Elba Sara hotel provided wonderful cocktails and tapas, a three course meal, wedding cake and an inclusive bar free until midnight at a fraction of what you would pay at a hotel in England. Fifty guests attended. The overall cost of the Wedding was £7000; for that standard it would have cost around £20,000 in England, which made the whole thing cost effective.

The big day arrives

They had a marvellous day but that wasn't the end of the work. The marriage certificate should have been given to them the next day, but it was a holiday in Spain, and as they were in England they collected this in October. They had to get a copy of the registry book entry, and have it translated into English by an approved translator, in order to change the brides name on her documents in England. In Spain ladies do not change their name on getting married. You get a book called a Libro de Famillia to record the details of your children. You need something similar when moving over here with children who will be attending school

Christmas in Fuerteventura, a guide to the festive season

Christmas in Fuerteventura begins only a couple of weeks earlier, not in September which is when it starts in England! Shops and houses put up decorations and Christmas trees much as we do at home. Although the shops get a little busier there isn't a mad rush to shop.

In Puerto del Rosario, there is a large nativity scene recreating life in Bethlehem. It is put up by the new bus station, a couple of weeks before Christmas in it is well worth walking round as some of the characters depicted are quite amusing. The lady in the photograph is doing her laundry by the river.

hristmas is a little mixed up over here. Father Christmas, or Papa Noel visits children on Christmas eve, but here he needs a ladder as there aren't any chimneys to climb down. Although Spanish children will probably get gifts from him too, the Spanish tradition is for children get their gifts in the early hours of the sixth of January on Dia de los

Reyes or Kings day. This is the day when the three kings arrived to give their gifts to baby Jesus.

The three kings arrive, strangely enough by ferry around 5pm on the evening of the fifth, and Melchor, Gaspar, Balthasar climb on their camels for a tour of the town, all the time throwing out sweets for the children (and adults). There is a huge scrabble around the floor to pick up the sweets.

It is traditional for Spanish children to leave their shoes outside filled with hay or carrots for the camels. Bad children get coal in stead of presents and you can buy sweets that look like coal if you feel like traumatising your children.

Large crowds wait for the kings, and at the end of the procession, the kings take letters from the children telling them what presents they would like when the kings visit their homes that night. It Puerto this was held by the Nativity Scene. The evening is good fun for all and everyone ends up with a big bag of sweets.

Christmas and Three king's day in Costa Caleta, Fuerteventura

On 5 January In Fuerteventura and the whole of Spain the end of Christmas is marked with a party. It is held in the evening prior to the day Spanish children get their Christmas presents, It celebrates the day that the Three Wise Men - Melchior Caspar and Balthazar arrived at the place where Jesus was born. As the Three Wise Men gave gifts to baby Jesus, here they share out presents amongst children; The Three Kings seem to be more popular in Spain than Father Christmas is!

At bedtime, as with Father Christmas in other traditions, children will put some milk and biscuits next to the Christmas tree for the Three Kings and some water for their camels. They also leave out their best pair of shoes to be filled with presents, rather than stockings.

On the next day, 6 January children wake up and see how many presents they have received. If they have been good, they will find a lot of good presents but if they have been naughty they will find coal. These days, the coal is actually made of sugar, and they might get some anyway, but some years ago it was real coal.

It is also traditional to enjoy a piece of roscon (a sugar-frosted fruit-filled bread) for breakfast tradition says that the person who finds a novelty such as a coin, in his or her piece will have good luck for the next year.

Sadly, despite the weather being superb over the last few weeks, this year's festivities in Caleta,, a planned a procession from the hotels near the Atlantico shopping centre to the center of Caleta had to be changed due to the weather turning to rain in the late afternoon, and the procession had to be cancelled. Of all the days for that to happen!

This was a greater shame as the BBC were filming it and the presenter Mike Bushell got quite wet whilst waiting to see what would happen. I have to say he took it very well and hung around in the rain whilst waiting to see what was happening. The event was moved to the Harbour where the children and their families managed to see the Three Kings indoors rather than in the open air.

There were similar events held in most towns but these would also have had to be changed due to the rain. The next day was hot and sunny again!

New Year's Eve was a fabulous night in Caleta with a free performance from a live band from Argentina. I can definitely recommend taking a Christmas break in the sunshine in Sunny Fuerteventura

Canarian Wrestling, Lucha Canaria on Fuerteventura

Canarian wrestling is a popular sport on Fuerteventura, and there are clubs in most of the towns. The sport goes back to the 15th century. The aim of the sport is to unbalance your opponent so that he is made to touch the ground with any part of the body other than the soles of the feet.

The bout is called an agarrada. The sport is very respectful, as the opponents went into the ring they touched the sand and crossed themselves. Then they greet each other by shaking hands. They then bend towards each other and grip the opponents right leg, then begin to force each other over.

There aren't any weight categories in Canarian wrestling, as opponents use skill to beat the opposition, not brute force. Fights last around 1 to 2 minutes. In classic competitions the team is made up of 12 wrestlers, with the best one technically and physically being called the Puntal, or cornerstone. The Mandador, who is the team leader and trainer will decide the order that the wrestlers go in to fight.

Visit a lava cave

The centre is open Tuesdays to Saturdays.

Tours are every 30 minutes from 10.15 to 12.45 and from 14.45 to 17.15.

Prices 5€ per person,
Children under 12 free.
Groups of 10 or more 3.75€ per person.
Residents 2.50€

Telephone 928 175 928

The cave is a million years old, and is the oldest in all the archipelago. It is home to an endemic arachnid, Maiorerus Randoi, and has a subterranean gallery that is 400m in length and 7 to 10m metres wide.

This visitor's centre, with almost 400m of accessible cave, is unique within the Canaries. The cave was constructed from a volcanic pipe of considerable dimensions, and is accessed via a large jameo (part of the tube whose roof has collapsed) divided into two branches. The north branch, which is larger and more inclined, is some 500 metres in length, and visitors can easily access some 400 metres of this branch.

Throughout its history man has put the cave to different uses. These include a corral for camels, a poultry coup and an arsenal. In recent decades the cave suffered a state of degradation that threatened the ecosystem of the cave.

Interesting Biology

In a study carried out by the Faculty of Biology of the Universidad de La Laguna unusual results were seen. Without doubt the most spectacular discovery was that of the opilionid (harvestman) Maiorerus randoi, an arachnid that does not spin a web. This species is exclusive to Cueva del Llano, which is the only cave on Fuerteventura with a suitable environment. It is also one of seven Canarian arachnids in danger of extinction.

Maiorerus randoi is an example of a species adapted to the eternal darkness of a subterranean life. As a result it has lost its pigmentation and is a yellowish colour. Its eyes, useless in the subterranean depths, have completely wasted away. This species is an example of what is sometimes called a living fossil, there being no other similar species in the Canaries. Its ancestors probably arrived on the archipelago in a former time when the climate was more humid.

Among the fauna of the volcanic pipe there are also other new species, Spernophorides fuertecavensis wunderlicht, another arachnid that is adapted to its environment, but not to the same extent as Maiorerus randoi. To ensure the conservation of both these species, along with others within the ecosystem, measures have been taken to restrict access to the areas where they live, as well as to control the humidity.

The southern branch is completely silted up, apart from a section excavated by the Cabildo. In this stretch there is an important paleontological site, rich in the remains of vertebrates and gastropod fossils and sub fossils.

Reasons for Creating the Centre
According to the president of the Cabildo, it is the importance of this section from a scientific and cultural point of view, together with the

rest of the cave that caused the Cabildo to go ahead with the creation of the museum. Valuing the possibilities to convert the site into an important cultural centre that would allow its visitors to have the opportunity to access the reconstruction of a very important part of the past of our islands.

He also says the result has been excellent, because the centre, importantly limited in its exterior construction, has been taken as a model of intervention in many international forums.

The primary objective is the protection of the cave. Before the Cabildo began to develop the museum, the cave was completely without protection, allowing indiscriminate visits, which could have had a serious effect on the fauna that lives there.

The Museum
Once the work was completed, the museum was developed in conjunction with experts in the field from the Cabildo of Tenerife.

The result is a museum based around four themes.

1 The geological history of Fuerteventura.
2 Volcanism and the formation of volcanic pipes.

3 The evolution of biodiversity on Fuerteventura.

4 Subterranean life endemic to the cave.

The project is based on a finca where the entrance to the cave is located. A Majorero style building has been created and the entrance to the cave has been created close to the jameo with a wall surrounding it.

The low building includes a foyer, an exhibition room, a gift shop, a cafeteria, toilets and stores, with a total area of 425 square metres.

Paleontological Interest

This cave is unique among the lava pipes of the Canaries. It is a special example, as it provides information about the general erosion of Fuerteventura, and has an abundance of animal fossils trapped in its sediments.

These remains mean that the site is one of paleontological interest, and among the lava pipes of the Canaries it has the greatest concentration of remains. The cave is a typical lava pipe that has functioned for thousands of years as the drain of a small water catchment. The successive streams of water that have poured in its interior have filled the cavity with sediments, and these have gradually reduced the length of the cave. The cave has in fact behaved as a subterranean ravine. Another distinguishing feature of the cave is its own existence, since the long erosive process that Fuerteventura has suffered has erased most of the volcanic structures of the island. Only some examples of the effects of the eruptions of the last four million years are conserved.

Fuerteventura's only Cave Ecosystem.

The cave is the only one in Fuerteventura that can harbour cave species. This is due to the high humidity and to the environmental stability, which in turn is a consequence of two circumstances: the location of its mouth in the valley, acting of drain of rain water, and the backfill of its cracks by clay, which impedes rapid evaporation.

The subterranean level has a poor ecosystem, due to the high environmental humidity and the absolute darkness. The animals that populate this level are, mostly, insects and arachnids adapted to live permanently in the darkness.

Geological Dimensions.

The cave is a million years old. It is a lava pipe whose length is 648 meters, although the last 200 prove difficult to explore, as they are almost plugged by sediments. The passable zone of the pipe is of considerable dimensions, with widths from 7 to 12 meters and heights between 3 and 5 meters. The slope is low, of barely a degree and the walls, worn by the passing of time, have tide marks of clay that indicate the different levels of flood that the cavity has suffered. There is another branch some 40 metres from the entrance that has been completely blocked by these sediments.

Geological History

The volcanic eruption that caused the Cave of the Plain has been a mystery for a long time. The pipe, as indicated its name, appears in the middle of a plain, (Cuevo de Lllanos means cave of the plains), without any apparent connection with some volcano or nearby eruption. The erosion, sedimentation and subsequent eruptions have erased the tracks of its development, and scientists have had to use indirect means to determine it origin of the cave.

It is the oldest zone on the island and represents the phase of underwater growth, which happened more than 20 million years ago, the oldest materials having an age of 70 million years and more. Geographically it is in the zone known as the Massif of Betancuria, where there have been other subsequent geological phenomena. These have helped construct the main nucleus of the island. Three main volcanoes with ages between 12 and 20 million years built the island. The main one, at Betancuria, surpassed 3.000 m in altitude. Nowadays the island is very eroded (the Betancuria Massif is only a few hundred metres high) and it is difficult to reconstruct the history of the island with accuracy and detail.

The geological data places the origin of the cave in the volcano of Mount Escanfraga, whose age surpasses 800.000 years. This age is calculated from the magnetic polarity rather than by the caliches (covering layers). The lavas of the cave and of Escanfraga have inverted polarity (the most recent inversion of terrestrial magnetism occurred some 800.000 years ago). Thehe nearby Cave of Villaverde has a normal polarity that suggests a later eruption that poured new lava over the lava arising from Mount Escanfraga.

A Lake of Lava

The cave is a volcanic pipe that was formed from a pool of lava that was emptied slowly. While the surface of the lake solidified, the liquid lava of the interior flowed away, leaving enormous empty spaces. The sediments that accumulated in the cave are the result of transportation from outside and the erosion of the walls of the pipe. Water and clay, as well as the remains of animals that today we see fossilised, were transported from the small catchment area.

Fossil Record

There are five phases of deposits that show how two humid periods have alternated with drier ones. The most humid epochs are detected by the abundance of species associated with humid conditions, as is the case of some terrestrial conches. The mollusc fossils of the first period have been dated to some 15.000 years, and the second to around 7.500 years.

The fossils of the Cave show Fuerteventura as an island that has had humid periods, with more vegetation, as indicated by some of the species found. The sediments have also conserved the remains of vertebrates that are extinct, such as the bobwhite canary (Coturnix gomerae) and the lava mouse (Malpaisomys insularis). Mammals, reptiles and birds are among the vertebrates appearing in the fossil register of the volcanic pipe, and most of the vertebrates found are the result of the feeding habits of other species, such as the common owl. Other remains have been carried to the cave in the water and clay.

Restaurants in Fuerteventura

There is a wide range of restaurants to be found on Fuerteventura, and it is unlikely that the national cuisine of any particular country is not represented somewhere in Fuerteventura.

Fuerteventuran Cuisine and Gastronomy

As Fuerteventura is an island that is surrounded by bountiful seas, a lot of the local cuisine is based on the fruits of the sea. Fish and seafood dishes are prominent, and the Spanish restaurants that have been on Fuerteventura for generations are expert in the creation of gastronomic delights based on the harvest of the sea. Other local dishes include Canarian potatoes, also called papas arragudas, which translates as wrinkled potatoes. These are small potatoes which were traditionally cooked in sea water, which being salty resulted in the wrinkled skin. They are served with mojo sauce, which comes in many varieties, the most common being a spicey red variety called mojo picante and a milder green version called mojo verde.

Spanish restaurants that serve the local cuisine as a speciality often have Tipico Canario on their menu and advertising.

English Cuisine

Many of the visitors to the island have very conservative tastes when it comes to their food, and some children have famously finickety food fads. There are many restaurants, especially in the North of the island, that cater for English tastes. English breakfasts are available in all the major resorts, and Sunday Lunches can also be found in great abundance.

All the restaurants will claim that they make the best Sunday Lunch on Fuerteventura, but in a fortnights holiday you will only be able to sample two.

Food for Global Gourmets

The population of Fuerteventura has increased in recent years and a list of the country of origin of the immigrants would be of considerable length. Besides those of us from Northern Europe, who have come here for a better climate a more relaxed way of life, there are many from South America, as well as Africa and Asia.

As catering accounts for a large chunk of the economic activity on the island, there are representatives from most nationalities within the sector, and the cuisine of a large number of countries provide the specialist section of many menus

Cruising around the Canaries

Each winter season the cruise ships visit Fuerteventura from around early October until mid April. Each winter sees an increase in cruise ship tourism as efforts to promote the island are made.

The most frequent visitors are the Aida group. Its a German based group, and during each weeks cruise their ship visits the islands of Madeira, La Palma, Fuerteventura, Lanzarote and Gran Canaria before returning to its starting point on Tenerife. The name of the ship visiting during 2011/12 is the Aida Sol, and can be seen in the cruise ship dock on Thursdays.

The Royal Artemis does a two week cruise starting from Southampton. Visiting Lisbon, Cadiz, Lanzarote, Fuerteventura Tenerife, Gran Canaria, Madiera and returning to Southampton.

The Kristina Regina route, visits seven of the Canary Islands in a one week cruise, going from Las Palmas - Puerto del Rosario - Arrecife - Santa Cruz de Tenerife - San Sebastian de la Gomera - Santa Cruz de la Palma -Puerta la Estaca - Las Palmas.

The Sea Clouds is a four-masted barque, sail ship, whose route begins at Santa Cruz/La Palma,visiting San Sebastian La Gomera, Arecife/Lanzarote, Rosario/Fuerteventura,and returning to Santa Cruz/Tenerife at the end of the week.

The Cabildo of Fuerteventura are working to make the most of the potential for this form of tourism, and the port of Puerto del Rosario is being developed so that it is better able to accommodate cruise ships.

Given a day in port it is possible to take part in a number of activities. Some of the tourists from the cruise ships travel around the islands capital on bicycles. There is a bus service, the number 17 that leaves from the gates of the port and calls in at Caleta de Fuste on its way to Gran Tarajal . It is also possible to take the regular bus services to other parts of the island. Other passengers go on Trike Tours, hire a car or go on organised tours.

Fuerteventura, Wildlife and Nature

Fuerteventura was declared a Biosphere Reserve in May 2009 because of it's rich and unique natural setting. There are three main areas:

Firstly, the east coast there are sand dunes, low cliffs and long beaches which are home to many endemic and rare species of plants and birds.

Secondly, the western coast has 100 km of high cliffs and isolated beaches.

Thirdly, the middle of the island has a large expanse of dry steppe and extinct volcanoes, and is the home of some rare birds like the Houbara Bustard, Egyptian Vulture and the Canary Island Chat, which is now only found on Fuerteventura.

All mammals on the island have been introduced either deliberately or accidentally. Goats roam over the barren land and feed off wild grasses, lichens and aromatic herbs. The goat meat and cheese is well renowned for it's flavour.

Also there are 13 protected natural areas on the island which cover just over 50% of the island, and the sea drops to 1 km very quickly off the coast of the island, and the sea is incredibly rich in marine life. Whilst the island, with it's volcanic origins, is very barren and there is a lack of trees and vegetation.

There's a wide range of birds to be spotted on the island, and these include Ruddy Shellduck, Mallard, Common Teal, Cattle Egret, Little Egret, Egptian Vulture ,Eurasion Spoonbill, Common Buzzard, Common Kestrel, Barbary Falcon, Moorhen ,Coot, Houbara Bustard, Black-winged Stilt ,Stone-curlew, Little Ringed Plover, Black-headed Gull, Eurasian C ollared Dove, Eurasian Hoopoe, Berthelot´s Pipet, Canary Island´s Stonechat, Southern Grey Shrike, Common Raven, Spanish Sparrow, Common Linnet and Trumpeter Finch.

The usual mammals to be seen are the Algerian Hedgehog, Barbary Ground Squirrel, Bats, Brown Rats, Mice and Rabbits.

Reptiles include Geckos and Lizards. I had two Geckos that each moved in to my apartment for a few days, one of them was huge! They moved around the room and were often found hanging frim the ceiling.

Butterflies include the Bath White, Greenish Black Tip, African Migrant, Cloudied Yellow, Geranium Bronze, Monarch and Painted Lady

Lanzarote

Lanzarote is only a short distance from Fuerteventura and the town of Playa Blanca can be seen gleaming white in the distance from Corralejo.

An ambitious plan to build a bridge linking Lanzarote and Fuerteventura so that it would be possible to travel by train between the north of Lanzarote and the south of Fuerteventura have been posited, but for the foreseeable future the only options involve crossing by boat or a very long swim.

The normal ferry journey takes between 25-40 minutes depending on the speed of the craft you are travelling on, whilst the fast ferry does the crossing in only twelve minutes. The ferries travel between Corralejo and Playa Blanca and it is possible to take a car from one island to the other. If you are using a hire car you need to check that you are covered by the insurance if you travel from one island to the other.

Tourists travelling from Fuerteventura to Lanzarote for one of the full day trips take in some or all of the major attractions, which are Timanfaya National park, Jameos del Agua, La Cueva de los Verdes, El Golfo, Los Hervideros, Castillo de San Gabriel, Casa Museo and the Monumento al Campesino.

Those coming from Lanzarote to Fuerteventura will find that there is plenty to do in and around Corralejo.

The Marina Rubicon is a large harbour, and is also the setting for water sports events, such as transatlantic races, fishing competitions, regattas, surfing competitions etc.

There is also a market held at the Marina Rubicon, only a kilometre away from the harbour, which is held on Wednesdays and Saturdays 9am to 2pm. Here you can buy the usual range of leather goods, clothing and souvenirs that you would expect on a Canarian market plus a few more unusual items.

There are a couple of beaches in Playa Blanca, but going to Lanzarote from Fuerteventura to visit its beaches, is pointless as Fuerteventura has enough beaches to keep even the most ardent beach lover happy.

Tour

2-Day Scuba Course with Open-Water Dive

Dive into the open waters of the Atlantic with a 2-day course that introduces you to the technique and spectacle of scuba diving. With a combination of theoretical and practical lessons, your PADI-certified guide introduces you to the wonders of exploring off the shores of Lanzarote.

Day 1: Theory & Pool Diving

You're picked up from your hotel for the ride to the dive center, where your guide introduces you to the world of scuba. A theoretical class teaches you the principles behind a successful dive, and then you get to try on the gear with an immersion in the onsite swimming pool. Hone your new skills in a controlled setting as you get ready for the real adventure ahead.

Day 2: Open-Water Diving

Your second day takes you to an ideal spot along the coast, chosen based on the day's weather conditions for calm, inviting waters, where your guide leads you into the sea. You can dive to depths of up to 19 feet (6 m) in the shallows and try out your newfound skills as you get to know the sea creatures who make Lanzarote's coast their home.

Local (toll-free) 1-866-310-5768

From abroad (charges apply): +1 404-728-8787

John Knight

Beginner Scuba Diving Lesson in Caleta de Fuste

Discover the incredible underwater world of Fuerteventura with a scuba diving lesson designed for beginners. With an expert instructor guiding the way, undergo a lesson in the swimming pool before diving into the ocean to see spectacular marine life such as red coral, loggerhead turtles, and schools of tropical fish.

Upon arrival at the dive center, you're greeted by your expert instructor who brings you into the world of scuba diving. The first part of your lesson involves the basics learning all about the equipment, hand signals, and safety rules. Next, you strap into your gear and take a plunge in the swimming pool. Spend some time getting comfortable with your equipment before making your way to the beach.

Once you're ready to dive, submerse yourself into the bright blue water just off the coast of Caleta da Fuste. At depths of up to 20 feet (6 m), get close to some of the region's most incredible sea life such as octopuses, sea turtles, starfish, and brightly colored triggerfish. Once back on land, enjoy access to a gallery of digital photos to commemorate your underwater adventure.

Local (toll-free) 1-866-310-5768

From abroad (charges apply): +1 404-728-8787

Catamaran Cruise to Playa de Papagayo

Board the luxurious catamaran *Catlanza* and sail to the beautiful beach of Playa de Papagayo on Lanzarote. Soak up the sun, watch for dolphins, and relax as you visit the remote gold-sand beaches of this paradisiac place.

On the way from Fuerteventura to Playa de Papagayo, you may spot dolphins or even whales. As you sail on the catamaran, relax, enjoy the sun, and sip a drink. Once in Papagayo, swim in the crystal-clear water or stroll on the beach and do nothing but admire the natural beauty. If you prefer an adrenaline rush, join a crew member for a ride on a jet ski.

If you want to improve your boating skills, take part in the maneuvers on the catamaran and help unfurl the sails or learn how to navigate. In the meantime the professional crew prepares a tasty lunch with fresh pasta and several sauces, bread, and salads. After lunch, sail back to the port of Puerto Calero and relax as you listen to the sound of the waves and feel the sea breeze.

Local (toll-free) 1-866-310-5768

From abroad (charges apply): +1 404-728-8787

Fuerteventura Oasis Park

Visit a huge natural reserve in the south of Fuerteventura to explore the variety of wildlife in Oasis Park. With more than 7,000 species of plants and animals from across Europe and beyond, including exotic and endangered species, the park truly is an oasis amid the island's arid landscape.

Explore the scenery at your own pace to find hidden nooks, shady corners, and spots to rest, relax, and admire the environment around you. The lush, 200-acre (80-ha) landscaped garden is full of colorful flora, and more than 2,300 different species of tropical plants and cacti make your surroundings one of the most diverse collections of its kind in Europe.

While you're there, you can see parrots perform a few surprising tricks and admire the skills and speed of falcons, eagles and owls. Children can get up close to rabbits, donkeys, turkeys, and swans, or try a ride around the farm on one of the 3 friendly ponies, to make some great memories for the whole family.
Local (toll-free) 1-866-310-5768
From abroad (charges apply): +1 404-728-8787

Freebird Catamaran Tour to Isla de Lobos

Enjoy a wonderful day sailing aboard a luxurious catamaran. With convenient pickup at your Corralejo hotel, this trip takes you from Corralejo to beautiful Lobos Island, or Isla de Lobos, a nature reserve.

One of the most beautiful places of the Canary Islands, Isla de Lobos is a safe haven for many species and a spot of unspoiled nature. As a matter of fact, the entire island is a nature reserve. This small island was named for the large number of sea wolves (*lobo marino*) that once lived there.

This excursion is ideal for people interested in seeing unspoiled nature and ecologists. Visit the many beaches and hidden bays, go for a swim, enjoy a bike ride, or explore the many hiking routes. Another highlight of Isla de Lobos is the Punta Martiño Lighthouse, perched on a hill along the northern end of this beautiful island.

With convenient roundtrip transportation to and from your Corralejo hotel, relax and enjoy a wonderful day in nature with your family or friends. Along the way, dine on delicious typical Canary Island food and beverages on this luxurious catamaran.
Local (toll-free) 1-866-310-5768
From abroad (charges apply): +1 404-728-8787

Full-Day Trip to Fuerteventura

Spend a wonderful day on Lanzarote's neighboring island, Fuerteventura. Be amazed by the immense contrasts between the two islands that are in very close proximity to one another. Enjoy the Dunes of Corralejo and have a delicious lunch among the locals.

Begin your tour with a convenient pickup from your hotel. Then, catch the modern ferry at the port of Playa Blanca and cruise across the water to Fuerteventura. Here, you can get to know an island full of contrasts and many charming small villages.

Explore the beautiful village of La Oliva in the north, and Tefia or Tiscamanita in the center. You can also visit Pájara a wonderful oasis in the middle of arid mountains and the old capital of the island, Betancuria.

The route continues along the coast to Fuerteventura's current capital, Puerto del Rosario. One of the last sites is the spectacular Natural Reserve Dunes of Coralejo. These dunes are truly a sight to marvel at and present you with outstanding photo opportunities. Snap plenty of photos before heading back to the port and returning to Lanzarote.
Local (toll-free) 1-866-310-5768
From abroad (charges apply): +1 404-728-8787

Full-Day Trip to Fuerteventura's Sand Dunes

Join this excursion to the Sand Dunes of the Corralejo Natural Park on the neighboring island of Fuerteventura. Enjoy a relaxing boat ride where you can take in the incredible sights along the coast of both islands. Then, feel like you are in the Sahara without ever leaving the Canary Islands.

Go to the port, where the glass-bottomed boat awaits to whisk you off to Fuerteventura. On the way there, look for dolphins or even whales through the underwater windows. Take time to stroll down the beautiful marina and the shopping street once you arrive at Corralejo. At noon, a bus takes you to a restaurant, where you can enjoy a savory lunch.

After having recharged your batteries, visit one of the highest sand dunes of this natural park. Don't miss the chance to take some amazing pictures before going back to the boat. On the way back to Lanzarote, the boat stops for you to see hidden wonders of the Atlantic Ocean through the glass-bottom windows.
Local (toll-free) 1-866-310-5768
From abroad (charges apply): +1 404-728-8787

Glass-Bottom Boat Cruise to 3 Islands

Enjoy a beautiful half-day cruise aboard a glass-bottom boat and feast your eyes upon the amazing coastlines of 3 islands including Fuerteventura, Lanzarote, and Isla de Lobos. Admire the white-sand beaches, take time to snorkel or sunbathe, and enjoy a lunch of Canary Island specialties.

After convenient pickup from your Corralejo hotel, this excursion takes you from Corralejo to Playa Blanca, or White Beach, in Lanzarote. Discover the seemingly endless white-sand beaches and opt to sunbathe and relax, go shopping, or stroll up and down the Marina Rubicon.

The next stage is at sea again. You have plenty of time to swim or snorkel with the equipment provided. Then your crew serves a traditional lunch with Canary Island specialties such as Canarian potatoes with a typical sauce, fresh fried fish, salad, fruit, and drinks.

Next, stop at Isla de Lobos and feast your eyes upon the magical underwater landscapes through the boat's glass bottom. See lots of fish, reefs, and if you are lucky, you may even spot dolphins. Once on the island, explore an incredible unspoiled nature reserve on foot, opt to sunbathe, or just relax before the boat takes you back to Corralejo. Local (toll-free) 1-866-310-5768
From abroad (charges apply): +1 404-728-8787

Glass-bottomed Sailing Adventure

Spend a day on one of the Canary Islands' most beautiful beaches with a scenic cruise aboard a glass-bottomed boat. Enjoy the views of the coast and admire the waters below the boat's windows on your way to a pristine section of tropical shore, where you can make the most of your adventure.

The Canary Islands are known for their beautiful, pristine beaches, and a trip to Papagayo Beach can show you why. Once you arrive at the scenic destination along Lanzarote's coast, you can take to the water for a swim, snorkel, go kayaking, or just sunbathe on the shore. Don't forget your camera, so you can take some spectacular pictures of your surroundings.

If you're up for something a little more active, you can try a ride on the banana boat or take a tour of the amazing white-sand beaches by speedboat. Dine on a delicious lunch and sip some sangria or a cold beer as you cruise back to Fuerteventura.

Local (toll-free) 1-866-310-5768
From abroad (charges apply): +1 404-728-8787

Go-Kart Experience at Gran Karting Club

Feel the rush of adrenaline as you speed your way around the largest go-kart track in all of Europe. Unleash your inner racecar driver as you zoom around a track for 8 electrifying minutes, traveling at speeds of up to 50 miles per hour (80 km/h).

Following pickup from your Lanzarote hotel, you're driven to the Gran Karting Club, one of the leading go-kart circuits in the world. Upon arrival, you're set up with your vehicle a 160cc Kart Honda for kids 10–15 or a 270cc Kart Senior for those over 16.

Once in your go-kart, put the pedal to the metal, zipping around a mile-long (1.5 km) track at up to 50 miles per hour (80 km/h). The young and those young at heart will relish the heart-pounding speed as they fly through the course for 8 unforgettable minutes.

Kids as young as 5 can get in on the action, too. On a smaller half-mile (900 m) track, those 5–9 can fill their need for speed as an on-site supervisor monitors the activity at all times to ensure the safety of the little ones.

Local (toll-free) 1-866-310-5768

From abroad (charges apply): +1 404-728-8787

Grand Tour of Lanzarote

Lanzarote is more than just beaches and hotels. It hides impressive volcanic landscapes, wonderful coasts, charming villages, vineyards, and aloe vera. Take a bus tour to discover the sights of this great island and enjoy a tasty lunch.

The first stage of this trip takes you to the Timanfaya National Park, a unique place shaped by volcanic eruptions. Visit the geothermic experiment facilities demonstrating the overwhelming power of the subterranean heat. Watch the geysers, steaming volcanic surfaces, and the spontaneous combustion of bushes.

Next, head to Los Hervideros and watch the sea flow in and out of volcanic tunnels, foaming up and painting the coast white. Visit the caves and the Green Lagoon at El Golfo. Treat your taste buds with lunch at Yaiza and then visit a wine cellar in the island's wine production region. Taste some of the superb wines and stop at an aloe vera farm to learn about the almost magical properties of the plant.

The last stage of this excursion takes you to Jameos del Agua, an ancient lava tunnel decorated by the local artist Cesar Manrique. Here you find a unique species, the blind crab. Then on your way back to your hotel, you pass Guatiza and Tahiche

Local (toll-free) 1-866-310-5768

From abroad (charges apply): +1 404-728-8787

Lobos Island Full-Day Tour with Lunch

Explore an island that was declared a nature reserve in 1982. See the untouched beauty that has been maintained by its protected status. From pristine beaches, to an ominous volcano, Lobos Island is a diverse wonderland. Enjoy free time to wander wherever your heart takes you.

Catch the ferry at Playa Blanca and enjoy the scenic ride to Fuerteventura where you meet your guide. Then, embark on another boat to Lobos Island perfectly situated between Lanzarote and Fuerteventura. Visit a small fisherman's village and delight in a lunch of fried fresh fish, Paella, or a local specialty of papas arrugadas with mojo sauce.

After lunch, use your free time to lie on the beach and soak up the sun, hike to La Caldera volcano, or visit the Punta Martiño lighthouse. Meet back up with your guide and share stories as you begin the journey back to Lanzarote.

Local (toll-free) 1-866-310-5768

From abroad (charges apply): +1 404-728-8787

Off-Road Safari along Fuerteventura's Northern Coast

Climb into a jeep and explore the most remote corners of the island with professional guides. With a chance to see rugged cliffs, a volcanic crater, and a pristine white-sand beach, this adventure is the safest and easiest way to get to know the least-known places of Fuerteventura.

Fasten your seat belt and let the adrenaline level get higher and higher. The experienced drivers show you the hidden off-road paths to extinct volcanoes, secluded beaches, charming villages, and canyons.

Meet your guide and driver at Villaverde and then head to Morros de Bayuyo, driving in dirt tracks and raising clouds of dust. Then you drive through a volcanic landscape full of the remnants of old eruptions emulating a Mars-like landscape. In Morros you have the chance to taste some products made from agave, the same plant used to make tequila.

Next, visit Tindaya and admire high rough cliffs facing the Atlantic. See the lighthouse El Tostón before speeding down to the white-sand beaches of El Cotillo to swim in crystal-clear water. In Lajares, enjoy lunch with some traditional dishes and recharge your batteries before the next stage of this safari leads you on foot to the crater of an inactive volcano. Then return to your hotel.

Local (toll-free) 1-866-310-5768

From abroad (charges apply): +1 404-728-8787

Off-Road Safari along Fuerteventura's Southern Coast

With a professional guide leading the way, get in a jeep and explore the most remote corners of the island. Visit the Jandia Nature Reserve, admire mountain views, seemingly endless beaches, and a charming village with stone houses.

Spend an unforgettable day visiting the Jandia Nature Reserve and the beautiful beaches of Cofete. After reaching Morro Jable, drive through dirt tracks to Punta de Jandia. Then your guide takes you to the mountains in the north and to Roque de Moro. Here, take in the spectacular views and feast your eyes on the coast and seemingly endless beaches.

The next stage takes you to Cofete, a small village with stone houses, where people still live a modest life without running water or electricity. Here, stop for a break before you head back to Punta de Jandia and its lighthouse. In this magical place enjoy a picnic on the beach before the convoy returns to Morro Jable.

Local (toll-free) 1-866-310-5768

From abroad (charges apply): +1 404-728-8787

Offshore Kayak & Snorkeling Adventure

See the unspoiled nature and peaceful turquoise waters of Fuerteventura's beautiful northern coast with this scenic kayak excursion. Paddle into the ocean for a look at this amazing place, and get the chance to jump in for a snorkeling dive to visit spectacular underwater caves.

Whatever your skill level, the excursion represents a great way to see the Canarian waters. Get settled on a sit-on-top kayak, ideal for exploring the coastal scenery thanks to its maneuverability and stability, and set out with a small group and a certified professional instructor to see what the ocean has in store.

Your 3 hours on the water give you a look at white sandy beaches and secluded coves, from the dunes at Corralejo Natural Park to the lagoons of El Cotillo. You can check out the sights beneath the surface as well, using the snorkeling gear to explore secluded locations that are best reached by sea.

Local (toll-free) 1-866-310-5768

From abroad (charges apply): +1 404-728-8787

Rancho Texas Lanzarote Park Admission

Spend your day in a western-style theme park on Lanzarote. The Rancho Texas Lanzarote Park is full of interesting animals like skunks, prairie dogs, armadillos, and raccoons. Enjoy the fun exhibits and feel like you've stepped into the Wild West, as you explore this unique park with your friends and family.

Begin your day by visiting some of the incredible exhibits and shows the park features. Watch the birds soar in the birds and prey or parrots and cockatoos shows. Or, take a peek at the lasso and whip exhibit. Don't miss the farm with the world's smallest animals and the best sea lion show on Lanzarote.

Next, go to the Indian village, medicine caves, and visit the Reptilarium filled with a lot of interesting cold-blooded animals. The park has species that you would typically find in the Americas including bison, cougars, and striped skunks. There are not only jaw-dropping animals to see and interact with, but also pools and waterslides and even a solarium.

Local (toll-free) 1-866-310-5768

From abroad (charges apply): +1 404-728-8787

Scuba Diving Introduction off the Lanzarote Coast

Discover the world of scuba diving along the shores of Lanzarote with an introductory course in the waters of Costa Teguise or Puerto del Carmen. An expert instructor gives you the chance to experience a whole new world under the waves of the Atlantic.

After a ride from your hotel, your instructors lead you to the shore for a quick orientation that gets you accustomed to your dive gear. Your dive location is chosen according to the sea conditions on the day, so take to the calm ocean and get used to breathing underwater as you experience the sense of weightlessness that comes while you're submerged.

The dives take you to depths up to 19 feet (6 m), where you can admire the fish around you and practice swimming in the shallow waters. Your guide is on hand to explain every step of the dive to you and offer any advice you need, so make the most of your time to learn a new, great way to explore.

Local (toll-free) 1-866-310-5768

From abroad (charges apply): +1 404-728-8787

Small-Group Cruise Aboard a Traditional Turkish Gulet

Spend a day sailing along Fuerteventura's beautiful southern coast aboard a traditional Turkish *gulet*. This traditionally built wooden ship offers a luxurious experience to a very limited number of passengers, letting you feel like a VIP as you relax on the water.

Your journey begins as the professional crew guides the grand sailing vessel out of the Morro Jable harbor, taking you south of Punta de Jandia and past the peaceful cliffs, secluded bays, and small fisherman's settlements along the coast. Relax in the tropical sun, feel the sea breeze, and enjoy the scenery with a cool drink in hand.

At the day's destination, you can jump in for a swim in the glittering blue waters south of Fuerteventura. Enjoy the views over the lighthouse on the top of the cliffs and dine on a delicious buffet lunch aboard the vessel before the cruise takes you back to Morro Jable
Local (toll-free) 1-866-310-5768
From abroad (charges apply): +1 404-728-8787

Ultimate Dune Buggy Adventure
Hop in a zippy dune buggy to cruise through the beachy landscapes and country roads of Fuerteventura. Rev the engine and feel the rush as you ride to remote beaches, speed toward a restaurant for a tasty lunch, and crisscross the island's ruggedly beautiful terrain.

After you're picked up from your hotel, ride to your starting point and get situated in your dune buggy, settling into the passenger seat or getting behind the wheel to control your ride. Once you're comfortable handling the buggy, set off after your guide from Costa Calma to La Lajita, where you can hop out to dig your toes into the sand, rest beneath palm trees, and watch local fishermen pulling in their boats.

From there, speed off through the Martian landscape of Tesejerague, letting the red dirt and dust fly on your way to Ajuy, a tiny village with a pristine and secluded black sand beach. Refuel over a tasty Mallorcan lunch in a restaurant, and then jump back in the buggy to make your way to Garvey. Spend some time at this lovely beach relaxing, swimming, and exploring a sea cave, and keep your eyes peeled for the remains of the *American Star*, a transatlantic ship that wrecked just offshore in 1994.

Begin your loop back, passing through Costa Calma to reach the Mirador del Sotavento, a promontory overlooking one of the island's most famous beaches. From here, gaze down at the crashing waves and shimmering teal waters where windsurfers and kite surfers compete before completing your exciting return ride to Costa Calma.

Local (toll-free) 1-866-310-5768

From abroad (charges apply): +1 404-728-8787

Submarine Tour

Dive below water in a submarine to explore the unknown depths of the ocean. See colorful swarms of fish, amazing reefs, and eerie shipwrecks through the large windows as you drop to a depth of 197 feet (60 m). Learn about the sub and the aquatic life from TV screens mounted throughout the ship.

Enjoy convenient pick up from your hotel and ride to the dock where your submarine awaits. After snapping a few pictures of the outside and receiving a brief safety orientation from the guide, climb inside and situation yourself in front of one of the huge windows. Hold your breath as the ship dives under the water and submerses you into a whole new world.

Watch as schools of fish swim by your window and remark on the many shapes, sizes, and colors of the diverse underwater population. Be amazed by the stunning coral reefs that stretch out along the ocean floors and keep an eye out for mysterious shipwrecked boats. With every system on the boat duplicated for safety, this is a perfect and safe way to have a once in a lifetime experience in Lanzarote.

Local (toll-free) 1-866-310-5768

From abroad (charges apply): +1 404-728-8787

Small-Group Fuerteventura Sightseeing Tour

Embark on a visually stunning tour of the heart of Fuerteventura, a true gem of the Canary Islands. Walk along easy footpaths that wind through this ancient area and learn about the island's sacred history, all in the company of a small group that helps create an intimate experience.

Once you're picked up from your hotel, take a relaxing drive to the center of Fuerteventura, where you're greeted by breathtaking natural landscapes and pristine coastal views. Pass by the towns of La Oliva, Tindaya, and Tefia, making a stop for coffee on a spectacular balcony designed by Canarian artist César Manrique. Continue to La Presa de la Peñita, a canyon with a 75-foot (23-m) dam and take a scenic walk along a footpath.

After enjoying some free time to explore a local town, hop back into the coach and head to Ajuy, where a beautiful black-sand beach waits to be explored. Walk along the sand and get a look at enormous sea caves dotting the coast before seeing some pre-Hispanic ruins at L'Atalayita, an indigenous village. On the way back to your hotel, make a final stop at the natural park of Las Dunas, where huge sand dunes slide into the crystal-clear ocean.

Local (toll-free) 1-866-310-5768

From abroad (charges apply): +1 404-728-8787

Other Information

Twinkle Trust Animal Aid

Jenny Billimore, the founder of Twinkle Trust, visited Fuerteventura for the first time in April 1995. On the complex where she stayed she was upset to find countless cats and kittens starving and suffering from cat flu.

Twinkle

On speaking to the complex owner she realised that nothing was being done either to control the cat population, or to alleviate the suffering of the sick and dying cats. She was concerned for all the cats, but in particular she fell in love with a young female cat that she named Twinkle. Jenny decided to come back for Twinkle and take her to England. Although she returned within a month with the documentation to take Twinkle home, Twinkle had caught cat flu and died after four days at the vets. It is in memory of Twinkle that the charity gets its name.

Starting the action

Jenny decided to return to Fuerteventura with a team of volunteer vets and helpers to sterilise the cat population, and to treat sick cats. The complex owner agreed to get the support of the authorities and to provide accommodation for their trip

She managed, after a lot of hard work, to get together a team of vets and helpers that since then have visited Fuerteventura twice a year. On one visit in October 2005 they expected to work with around 100 cats, but actually, around 350 cats were treated in a week by the team, mainly for neutering, but also for other ailments such as cancer, which can affect the noses or ears of white cats in particular. You can identify cats that have been neutered by the trust as they cut off the tip of the left ear so that the cats will not be caught again unnecessarily.

£3,500 and £4,000 per trip

As you can imagine, although Jenny and the vets and helpers work on a voluntary basis, cages, cat food, cat litter, medical supplies, hire cars, and petrol are very expensive, and funding is hard to come by. Each cat has to be caught by a volunteer and brought to her animal hospital and returned after recovery. Each trip is more expensive than the last and costs between £3,500 and £4,000!

Friend of Twinkle Trust

If you would like to support Twinkle Trust, you could become a "Friend of Twinkle". An annual donation of £20 per year, or any other amount, could be put towards the drugs required to give the cats a more comfortable life. It could provide a cat cafe, where cats can be fed and given much needed fresh water.

Offer to help

Twinkle Trust does a valuable job to maintain the welfare of the many cats on the island. Twinkle Trust are looking for volunteers, either on Fuerteventura or from other places, to help during the twice-yearly visits. Volunteers get free accommodation, but have to fund other expenses themselves. Jenny would love to have contacts in each resort on Fuerteventura, who could transport a sick or injured cat to the vets. Alternatively you could foster a cat for a short time whilst it recovers from illness or an operation. Any offer that you could make would be appreciated. Please contact her if you would like to know more, or if you feel you could offer practical or financial support.

Contact details

Contact Twinkle Trust on 659 598 719 Fuerteventura

or in England 0044 208 688 9073,

or visit www.twinkletrust.org.

Twinkle Trust is a registered charity in England, no 1091253 and is an official member of the World Society for the Protection of Animals.(W.S.P.A.). They would like to thank Touricomplex and the Barcelo Hotel for providing free accommodation for the teams twice a year

Health Matters on Fuerteventura

Travel Insurance
When going on holiday it is really important that you take out good travel insurance. Anyone c an get ill, and you need to be prepared. Your E111 will allow you to have emergency treatment in hospital, but this may not be with an English speaking doctor and so you may have difficulty putting across your symptoms.

If you are taken ill, but it is not an emergency, you will need to see a GP. The initial consultation will cost about €90 but, with good travel insurance the GP should be able to contact your insurance company and take this direct from them rather than you having to pay out of your pocket. You must check if your policy has an excess though ,as you will have to pay that yourself.

Needing a GP

Clinic Dr Bludau

The medical clinic is situated in Caleta de Fuste, just next to the petrol station and opposite the Atlantico shopping centre. There are 2 doctors in the clinic full time - Dr Hans-Bernd Bludau, consultant in Internal Medicine and Dr Elaine Theaker.

They are open Monday to Friday 10am to 2pm, but a doctor is on-call 24/7 for emergencies and will do house calls if necessary.

They provide a wide variety of facilities and options to help you take the best care of yourself whilst you are on the island. Within the clinic they provide consultations in general medicine, internal medicine, general practice and emergencies. They have a small laboratory where they can perform general blood tests (such as full blood count, kidney function, liver function and heart enzymes), ultrasound (to check the abdomen, blood vessels and heart), ECG (normal and 24 hour), blood pressure monitoring, pulse wave analysis, lung function tests and can also send blood, swabs and samples to the main laboratory in the city.

They also provide services including psychotherapy, acupuncture and minor surgery. In addition, there is a dermatology clinic once a week with Dr Norbert Kuner, a gynaecology clinic once a month with Dr Katrin Gortner, paediatric advice and review with Dr Karola Simoni (Costa Calma), a physiotherapist (Anika Werner, PhysioRelax) who visits once a week and Deepak does Ayurvedic massage on demand. If you have any medical concerns, please phone them and they will do their best to treat you promptly in the clinic, however if you require other specialist services they can contact one of their professional colleagues as necessary.

Disabled Access
Recent legislation has meant that new public buildings have to be built with facilities to allow access to disabled users. An example is the new Las Rotundas shopping Cente in Puerto Del Rosario, which has ramp escalators.

Older buildings have had to be adapted so that ramps allow wheelchair access and it is noticeable that this has been done. Ramps have been added to older buildings, but since the design did not include the facility in the first place a small number of the ramps are interestingly steep. In some places, such as the Cocosol complex in Costa Antigua, which has 112 bungalows, were built in such a way that they were easily adapted to meet the needs of wheelchair users. If you need any mobility equipment please contact Miraflor Mobility.

Health Threats
The main threats to health on Fuerteventura, whether you are a holidaymaker, or have decided to live here, are the sun, alcohol and smoking.

It is very important to realise that the cooling effect of any wind that is blowing on Fuerteventura has no bearing on the ability of the sun to cause damage to your skin. In the busy summer holiday period the doctors in the resort are kept busy dealing with the immediate effects that the sun has on those that do not treat it with respect. If yo do not want to spend any of your valuable holiday in a doctor's waiting room than you should bear these points in mind.

Sun
The sun is at its highest and therefore strongest from noon - 4pm in the summer and 11am - 3pm in the winter. It is sensible to avoid being out in the sun between these times.

The sun is higher in the sky in Fuerteventura than it is in northern Europe. This means that shoulders and tops of heads as well as feet are more likely to catch the sun.

You don't have to be sunbathing to be affected by the suns harmful rays. Protection is needed whenever you are out and about.
High factor sun creams are not designed to allow you to stay out in the sun longer.

Alcohol
The indirect effects of drinking too much can be as damaging as the direct effects, particularly if you are on holiday. The high tempeatures

have a dehydrating effect as does drinking alcohol, so drinking alcohol to quench your thirst will not help to keep you hydrated. If you are thirsty you should drink water.

A couple or four pints at lunchtime will probably mean that you will want a nap. Many people have a nap in the sun and get burned, while others are less security conscious and forget to take due care of their property.

Shorts are served in larger measures than in the UK and this makes it harder to keep track of how much you have drunk. When you are at home you know the route from the bar to your bed well. When you are on holiday you don't, and this makes it more likely that you will trip and hurt yourself.

Smoking
Cigarettes are cheaper in Fuerteventura than in the UK, so it costs less to kill yourself. Since 2 January 2011, smoking is restricted in every indoor public place, including restaurants, bars and cafes.

Fuerteventura Transport

Fuerteventura is around 100km in length and ranges in width from about 5km to 30km. This relatively small size means that it is possible to comfortably visit anywhere on the island and return to your base in the same day.

Buses or Guaguas
The bus services on Fuerteventura have changed quite a bit recently so we have decided to do a full page of information to cover this.

There are some sixteen different bus routes on the island. The buses run to time and are an excellent way to get around the island. It takes about 20 minutes to travel by bus from Caleta de Fuste to Puerto del Rosario, and the travel time from Puerto del Rosario to Corralejo is around 40 minutes.

Full details of the timetable can be reached by clicking on the bus to the right. This will take you to the bus company's website.

If you travel around on buses quite often you can get a discount card which gives a discount of 30% off each journey. It is available on all bus routes on the island.

The Bono BtF (Discount Bus Card) is a rechargeable plastic card which can be bought from the bus driver. The card costs 1 euro and then you can charge it up with any amount from 15 euros to 50 euros in amounts of 5 euros. The driver gives you a receipt for the amount as well.

The big advantage is that the card can be bought from the driver, which is useful to holidaymakers as you can get discounted travel straight away.

With the card you state your destination to the driver, and put your card on the sensor in front of the driver. Your card is then debited. The same card can be used by several people and is transferable.

Taxis
Taxi's are quite cheap on the island, but you must remember that you cannot order them in advance, nor can the taxi's pick up passengers outside their own area, eg a Puerto taxi cannot pick up in Caleta.

The table below shows the cost of a taxi to various places on Fuerteventura fromFuerteventura Airport.Prices are a guide as it will depend on your exact destination.

Prices correct January 2017

Destination	Working days 06.00 - 20.00	20.00 - 06.00 and Sundays and Festival Days
Caleta de Fuste / Costa Caleta / El Castillo	€14.00	€15.00
Nuevo Horizonte / Costa Antigua	€11.00	€12.00

Corralejo	€46.00	€52.00
Costa Calma	€76.00	€86.00
El Cotillo	€52.00	€59.00
Origo Mare	€55.00	€59.00
Morro Jable / Playa Jandia	€97.00	€110.00
Costa Calma	€76.00	€81.00

Travelling by Car

The roads linking the main population centres on the island are generally of a high quality. Some of them, such as that from Costa Antigua to the town of Antigua are very new and do not appear on most maps.

The islands probably has more miles of tracks than tarmacced surfaces. It is possible to negotiate a lot of them with care, but if you have taken the car hire option , then you should be aware that your insurance may not be valid if you are anywhere other than on a "proper" road.

Ferry Services

The ferries that run between Fuerteventura and some of the other islands are more about getting to or from the island. You can find the timetables by following the links to the right.

Trains

Trains?, what trains? The closest thing to a train on the island are the tourist trains like the one that travels up and down Chipmunk Mountain, and over to the Atlantico Centre, There is also a tourist train in Corralejo.

Camels

When the first intrepid tourists arrived on the island, going to Corralejo involved a six hour camel ride. In Caleta there are couple of camels that will take you there and back! You can also ride a camel at the La Lajita zoo.

Emergencies

- Emergency Services 112
- Guardia Civil: 062
- Hospital:928 86 20 00
- Fire Brigade: 080
- Police: Antigua 928 87 80 24
- Police: Corralejo 928 86 61 07
- Police: Costa Calma 928 87 51 72
- Police: Morro Jable 928 50 10 22
- Police: Pajara 928 26 11 58

- Police: Puerto del Rosario 928 85 06 35
- Police: Tuineje 928 87 00 00
- Police: (Beach vigilance) 929 25 09 96
- Police: (Fishing) 989 35 13 80
- Red Cross: (Puerto del Rosario) 928 85 13 76

Taxis
- Puerto del Rosario 928 850 216
- Antigua (caleta de Fuste) 928 878 011
- La Oliva (Corralejo) 928 866 108
- Pajara (Morro Jable) 928 541 257
- Pajara (Costa Calma) 928 547 032
- Tuineje (Gran Tarajal) 928 870 059 + 928 870 737

Religious centres
Rectories
- Puerto del Rosario 928 850519
- Casillas del Angel (Tetir) 928 538 060
- Antigua-Betancuria 928 878 003
- La Oliva 928 161 457
- Pajara 928 161 457

- Tuineje 928 164 017
- Gran Tarajal 928 870 086
- Morro Jable 928 541 532

Churches

- Faros Christian Fellowship. Tel 697 470 220. English speaking evangelical church, with meetings in Corralejo, Calle Pizarro No8.
- Christian Evangelical Church, Puerto del Rosario. 928 532 684
- Evangelical Church of God, Puerto del Rosario. 928 532 564Puerto del Rosario. 928 532 684
- Evangelical Church Puerto del Rosario. 928 850 097
- Jehovah's Witnesses Puerto del Rosario. 928 531 580

Holidays for those with mobility and other disabilities in Fuerteventura.

Fuerteventura is a better holiday venue for those with Mobility problems than the other Canary Islands that I have visited. The reason for this is that the holiday resorts of Corralejo, Caleta, Costa Calma and Morro Jable are situated on an area of coastline which is relatively flat, where as some of the resorts on other islands tend to have an extremely steep climb up to the hotels. Fuerteventura's mountains tend to be located in the middle of the island.

Complying with the Disability Discrimination Act

Since the Disability Discrimination Act of 2004 came into force any amenity that has been built has had to comply with the law and all of the resorts have seen a lot of development since that time. Lots of the shops and bars are located together making access easiy for those with limited walking, and there are also several big shopping centres that are also disability friendly.

Mobility Hire

Another thing that makes Fuerteventua disability friendly, is that if you have a mobility problem you can take advantage of the way things have developed, and explore the resorts more fully by hiring one of the latest models of mobility scooter from a company such as Miraflor Mobility who can deliver items to suit your mobility needs to the main resorts of Corralejo, Caleta, Costa Calma and Jandia or any other location on Fuerteventura.

Touring on Fuerteventura.

Fuerteventura offers lots of scope for day trips by car, bus or even walking. It is well worth going out to visit different places as each part of the island differs so much.

When we did the trips, we were working. A tough job but somebody has to do it! With a little planning, most of the trips can be converted into a relaxing day out, and you can take time to explore all the variety and beauty Fuerteventura has to offer. The obvious attractions are the 125 different Fuerteventura beaches, such as those in Jandia, to the smaller more interesting beaches such as the one by the caves ofAjuy

Hiring a car.

It is easy to drive in Fuerteventura as the roads are laid out to make it simple, even when you are only used to driving on the left! Altough the islands are getting busier the roads are usually clear. They are in the process of completing new motorways too. Getting to the more secluded beaches involves driving down tracks., It is probably best to hire a four wheel drive vehicle, although we did these tours by car. If using a hire car, you may not be insured off road, so it's best to check the terms and conditions of your car hire company.

Touring by bus.

The buses here are very reliable and there are about 16 different bus routes on the island. Traveling on the bus is quite cheap and you can get tickets that give 10% discount. We have found the bus drivers to be friendly, and the cost of fares is usually on the side of the door as you enter the bus. See the Getting about page for details. The bus timetables are on the right.

Long Term Accommodation Fuerteventura

If you are thinking of moving to Fuerteventura to set up a new life then you will need somewhere to live. Buying a property is one option, but as new resident on the island you cannot be sure where you will end up working, or exactly what you need from a property. Property prices are relatively steady at the moment and the taxes involved in buying and selling property here mean that flitting from one place to another could prove to be expensive.

Besides not being able to be certain exactly where you will make your new life, there are many families that move out and then return home because one or more of them becomes homesick or finds that Fuerteventura is not what they thought it would be.

There is a lot of choice Fuerteventura because there has been a lot of building in recent years and much of this was snapped up by people looking for an investment or a holiday home. Property prices here are still below those on Lanzarote, Gran Canaria and Tenerife, and at the moment they are not rising, so the pressure to buy in a rising market is not there like it was a couple of years ago.

Approximate Cost of Accommodation.

Prices in the centre of the resorts on the island are higher than properties on the outskirts. If you want to be located in an area with a high percentage of English speakers, Parque Holandes, located between Corralejo and Puerto del Rosario, Tamaragua just outside Corralejo and Costa Antigua just outside of Caleta are probably the lowest priced options in the north of the island at the moment.

In Parque Holandes you can rent a three bedroom property for €500 including bills, whereas a one bedroom apartment in Costa Antigua costs about €300.

Typical prices in Corralejo would be a two bedroom property for €450 including bills and a two bedrooom townhouse in Caleta from €450 including bills.

Rental Contracts and Deposits

In general the law in Spain is weighted in favour of tenants who have a long term contract, so most landlords offer short term contracts, You will probably be offered a contract for three months. This can be renewed if the owner and yourselves agree. Probably you will be asked to pay a months rental in advance and a month as security. You should check with the owner if your property is included in the insurance that the owner has on the property. If not you should arrange your own.

It is worth checking to whether or not Utility bills are included in the monthly rental, and if it is not you should expect to pay about €40 for water and electricity per month

You can expect to have to pay a deposit equivalent to about one month's rent, and this should be returned at the end of the tenancy, as long as there is not an unreasonable amount of wear and tear.

General Information

Many properties for rental are on complexes that used to be rented out to holiday makers but have now been sold off. On these complexes there may be additional communal facilities such as swimming pools, gyms etc which are included in the price. There may also a be a lively bar that isn't so bad during a weeks holiday, but a little too much if you are living on the complex.

Houses in the tourist resorts will be referred to as villas, and will either have pools of their own and/or a community pool. Maintenance of the private pools will proably be included in the price as will garden maintenance. You should ask for the telephone numbers for recommended maintenance people in case you have need of their services.

You should also check if you need to bring your own towels and bedding or if these are supplied by the owners of the property.

Travel Information

FUERTEVENTURA TRAVEL INFORMATION

Where

Fuerteventura, located at Latitude 28° 27' N Longitude 13° 51' W, is the second largest island of the Canaries, measuring 110 km (75 miles) from north to south, and 20 km (15 miles) at its widest point with a surface area of 1600 sq km (620 sq miles). Its name derives from the Spanish for 'Strong wind'- for the north east trade winds blow strongly across the island for most of the year. Its closest neighbour is Lanzarote, some 10 kilometres (7 miles) the north and Gran Canaria 80 kilometres (50 miles) to the west. The west coast of Morocco is 100 km (60 miles) to the east.

Getting there

By ferry:

There are regular ferry services from Lanzarote (20 minutes on the high speed ferry from Corralejos), Tenerife (7 hours from Morro Jable) and Gran Canaria, (7 hours from Morro Jable).

By plane:

Easyjet now have scheduled flights from Liverpool to Fuerteventura on Monday, Wednesday and Saturday, and from Stansted to Fuerteventura on Wednesday and Saturday. Monarch airlines have weekly flights to Fuerteventura from Manchester, Birmingham, Gatwick and Luton on Wednesdays. There are also charter flights from major UK cities including Manchester and Liverpool. There are frequent interisland flights to the other main islands of the archipelago from the international El Matorral airport.

Getting around

By bus:

There are regular buses between Corralejos and Morro Jable but getting to smaller villages off the main north south axis can take time and services are infrequent.

By car:

There are a wide selection of car hire agencies at the airport and in the larger towns on the island. 4 x 4 jeeps and land cruisers are available for hire as many of the roads and tracks in the remoter parts and the natural parks of the island are unsurfaced. Do remember not to drive off marked tracks in Natural Parks, and that soft sand can be treacherous! Remember also that driving is on the right hand side.

Public holidays
- 1 January - New Year's Day
- 6 January - Epiphany
- March/April Good Friday
- 1 May - Labour Day
- 30 May - Day of the Community - Canaries Day
- 24 June - St. Johns Day
- 15 August - Assumption - Asunción
- 20 September - Our Lady of La Peña
- 1 November - All Saints' Day
- 6 December - Constitution Day
- 8 December - Immaculate Conception
- 25 December - Christmas Day

Weather

Fuerteventura has more than 3000 hours of sunshine per year and an average annual temperature of a balmy 22 degrees. Rain is very rare but is most likely between October and March. The trade winds blow from the north east most of the year ensuring that even the hottest of days will feel cool and pleasant. The Calima however - a hot dry wind from the east occasionally brings heat and dust from the Sahara - with temperatures that can rise over 40 degrees. Sea temperatures range from 18 degrees in January to 23 degrees in October.

Travelling with children

Fuerteventura is a perfect family holiday destination. Local people dote on children and are very family orientated - and you will see small children out with their parents late into the evening. Crime is rare in nearly all towns and villages and there is in general a warm and welcoming friendly atmosphere. Most of the beaches on the east coast have shallow, calm waters perfect for learning to swim. Larger beaches have lifeguards and flags clearly marking safe areas for swimming.

Electricity

230V AC, 50 Hz; European round two pin plugs are standard.

Dialling code

+34

Money

Euro

Time zone

The same as the UK - both GMT and BST

Events in Fuerteventura

Events on Fuerteventura, from a kitesurfing championship to an international jazz festival...

February/ March

Fuerteventura Wave Classic Windsurf Championships are held at Cotillo.

March

Carnival is celebrated throughout the island with fancy dress parades, processions of elaborately decorated floats and fancy dress completions

The annual Blues festival in Corralejo.

May

The Feria de Artesania is one of the most popular annual events on the island - with displays of locally made produce, from furniture to musical instruments, from the best local cheese to dried fish and clothing, painting and weaving. It is a good place too to listen to local musicians - and visiting groups from the other islands of the archipelago who come to play here in concerts held in the evenings. The 3 day Feria takes place in May at the central town of Antigua, and most islanders will come to visit the festival.

30th May: Canaries day on the 30th May to celebrate the first session of the autonomous government of the Canaries in May 1983. Celebrations are held in various towns and villages - the largest being in the administrative capital of Puerto Rosario.

July

14th : Saint Buenaventura day in Betancuria to celebrate the island's patron saint . Local cultural groups and musicians put on concerts and there is a procession through the historic old town.

Corralejo: The saint's day of Señora del Carmen the patron saint of Corralejo. A festival of dance, music and gastronomy with processions through the town.

Kiteboarding and windsurfing world and speed championships take place at Playa Sotavento near Costa Calma. Top riders from all over the world participate in the events which draw many international spectators.

August

Round the island kayak tour. This annual event - which is not a race - takes place over a week with many international visitors taking part. Its intention is to celebrate the beauty and marine diversity of the island's varied coastline.

September

The International Jazz festival takes place in Corralejo - with many international stars playing at the event.

On the third Thursday the festival of the Romería de la Peña in Vega de Río de Palmas. This celebrates the first European settlement in the

Atlantic here in 1404 - and the miraculous appearance of the vision of the Virgin . The most important festival on the island draws thousands of Majoreros on a pilgrimage to the village and the ravine where the vision took place.

Gran Tarajal: The international Open Deep Water Game Fishing Competition takes place offshore with international sport fishermen participating. Blue Marlin and big tuna are amongst the prize catches.

October

The annual swimming race to the Isla de los Lobos - 3.5 kilometres off the coast from Corralejo.

www.ingramcontent.com/pod-product-compliance
Lightning Source LLC
Chambersburg PA
CBHW021109080526
44587CB00010B/448